Confident Me

THE CONFIDENCE TOOLKIT FOR TEENS

NIKKI SALT

SARAH SCRASE-HOLLAMBY

KEVIN MAYHEW PUBLISHERS

Published in 2022 by Kevin Mayhew Ltd,
Fengate Farm,
Rattlesden,
Bury St Edmunds,
Suffolk, IP30 0SZ

Copyright © 2022 by Nikki Salt & Sarah Scrase-Hollamby
ISBN (paperback): 9781838581374
ISBN (eBook): 9781838581381
Paperback product code: 1501712
eBook product code: 1501713
All rights reserved.

Contents

Introduction

Dear Reader,

We have been working with children and teens for most of our lives and are repeatedly struck by how wonderful, thoughtful, kind and caring you young people are today. You seem to have a real heart for humankind, animals and the environment, more so than we ever remember as teens.

Yet, every day we see you suffer from lack of confidence, self-esteem and even self-hatred. You have grown up in a digital age that has so many positives and opportunities but it also has a sinister side. Now, more than ever before, you talk about being judged, you have enormous expectations of yourselves and are constantly comparing yourselves to impossibly high standards.

We decided to write a simple and truthful guide to help you navigate some of the trickier parts of growing up, especially through the teen years, by sharing stories and experiences that might just help you realise you are not alone, and you are actually very normal for having all of these questions, worries and doubts.

Life has its complications at the best of times, and going through puberty and piloting your way through realms of emotions, feelings, decisions, beliefs and opinions...well, sometimes you just need to press the pause button and check in. Hopefully, this book will be a comfort as well as an information tool. It will be a breath of freshness that is real and honest, and though at times raw, it will help you to recognise you are unique, perfectly designed and very much loved.

Nikki and Sarah

Deep down you know something isn't quite right,
You're struggling to find the strength to fight.
Another day full of fear,
With glazed over eyes, nothing is clear.
How can you escape when you are in your own prison?
And every second more negative thoughts have arisen.
Tossing and turning until 4am,
Checking the time again and again.
The monsters are inside of you, ridding you of hope,
You don't know how much longer you can cope.

Staring at your reflection in the mirror,
Criticising every flaw, picking up every error.
You're fed up of being in this unhealthy mindset,
Only seeing the situation's danger or threat.
You cannot accept compliments or praise,
Because all you can hear are voices, putting you in a daze.

Trust me I've been there, and I know how you feel,
But you've got to take time and let yourself heal.
Still some days I wake up, don't want to get out of bed,
Conquer my fears and face the day ahead.
Still some days I don't like what I see,
When I look in the mirror; but trust me, please.

You are worthy and you are loved,
You are brave and strong enough.
You have the power to tell yourself no,
When you feel like you've hit an all-time low.
There's no need to be ashamed to say how you feel,
Reach out for support and not keep everything concealed.
Don't beat yourself up for being a burden,
This anxiety is difficult, and you are just learning.
I promise if you've determined, you'll rise from the rubble,
You can find a light at the end of the tunnel.

- BY HARRIET AGED 13 -

CHAPTER 1
My Body

OUR BODY CONFIDENCE is formed by what we think and feel about our body. We might have the most perfect body, but if we don't believe it, then we may as well not have it. The truth is, most of us will focus on the negative whether this is due to our own perception or an unhelpful comment. And even if a friend compliments us, it's the negative stuff that sticks and can become magnified. Take Emma, for example: she suffers from acne and despite possessing one of those lovely faces where everything is in proportion, she only sees her spots. She thinks she's ugly.

Our confidence levels fluctuate, and just a simple throw away remark can have serious consequences of self-doubt. In our society it has become a habit for us to be negative about ourselves as a way of being modest. Even if someone compliments us, we can feel embarrassed and find an excuse for looking good.

. . .

"You look nice today."

"Oh, it's probably because I've washed my hair."

We constantly talk about our diets and proclaim cake as being 'bad' and fruit being 'good'. Some people will even go as far as to boast about missing meals. Society's perception that 'skinny is beautiful and fat is ugly' is harmful and downright wrong. Some people have become extremely ill in their quest to be thin, and later in this chapter, Eleanor will share her story about her battle with anorexia. This constant condemnation of ourselves does nothing to boost our confidence.

As we grow into adulthood we feel a need to be accepted by society. Our perceived failure to do this can result in harmful behaviour and can have quite serious consequences to our wellbeing. How many people do you know who settle for simply surviving another day at school? For getting through the day unnoticed?

Unfortunately school is a breeding ground for negative input. The charity, Youth Sight* surveyed more than 1000 secondary school pupils and discovered that not only were 55% of pupils being bullied about their appearance (mainly body size) but over half of these occurrences were by 'friends'!

I'm sure our 'friends' don't mean to be heartlessly cruel. In fact, the chances are they are also insecure about their own bodies. The truth is everyone has hang ups. Everyone is afraid of rejection, but we were not placed onto this earth to live in fear of rejection. Life is out there and should be lived!

. . .

You have a great future ahead of you. You are going places. Whatever your body hang-up; shape, size, ability, skin type… don't let it define you.

*Between 2017 and 2018, a research study survey of more than 1000 secondary school pupils aged from 11 to 16 was conducted by Youth Sight. They found that 55% of pupils were bullied about their appearance, most prominently for body shape and size. This resulted in over half of those bullied suffering from anxiety and over two thirds attempting to change their shape / size through dieting or increased exercise.

NUGGET OF TRUTH

Whatever your body hang-up; shape, size, ability, skin type... don't let it define you. You are so much more than that.

SARAH'S STORY

I loved the whole experience of my prom. The dress shopping and the chance to get my hair and nails done by professionals gave me a sense of feeling special, even glamorous. I think I can probably count on one hand the times I have felt genuinely 100% confident with my appearance, my weight and my body like that. I felt good. I didn't have a boyfriend at the time, but I had an older good friend (who happened to be rather fit) and he said that he would come to my prom with me. Result. Walking in with a 'hot' guy on my arm was hilarious. It was as though the room went silent and jaws dropped. How could Sarah pull a date like that? At that moment, my body confidence was at an all-time high, partly because of the dress, hair and make-up but partly because of who was on my arm.

More than anything at prom, I wanted to be accepted and even admired. I wanted people to look at me and think I had amazing hair, make-up and a good-looking date on my arm. But, later, when the dress was off, make-up removed, my PJs on and the 72 hairpins painstakingly removed from my head, I was left with me – the real, raw, and true me – and do you know what? For a moment, I realised that should be enough.

Don't get me wrong, I loved feeling confident, loved the affirmation from others, the dress, make-up and the professionally styled hair – who doesn't? But ultimately, my confidence needed to be rooted in the knowledge that I (without all the fluff and stuff) am enough. That God is the artist, the designer, the creator – the One who doesn't make mistakes – and when I look into the mirror, I can look beyond the imperfections. God created me in His image, and in that reflection, there are parts of Him. I am not a practice sketch or a doodle, I am His breath-taking masterpiece. There is an old song written back in the 80's (I know it's old but give it a chance) by a Canadian song writer that reminds me of this truth.

What I Am In You – Words & Music by Johnny Markin (used with permission)

> *Passing by a mirror just the other day*
> *I saw myself in a very different way*
> *Stripped of all the coverings*
> *That hide reality*
> *Removed from all the many roles I play*

> *There wasn't anything that I could hide from you*
> *And for the moment there was nothing I could do*
> *For the eyes that searched my heart*
> *Were of the one who saved my soul*
> *And Jesus, you revealed to me this truth… that…*

What I am in You is what I am… ©1986 Rare Bear Music

SELF-JUDGEMENT

We are judged so much by what we wear, how we look and who is on our arm, and if we're not careful it consumes our thinking.

But if we were to stand back and observe our thoughts during an average day, most of us would see a fair share of self-judgement, as well as judgement coming from others.

Try and think about your day today – how many times have you had negative or judgemental thoughts about yourself? According to a research conducted by the National Science Foundation, around 80% of our thoughts are negative. And we have approximately 12,000 - 50,000 thoughts daily. Wow! I'm not particularly good at maths but even I know that is not a favourable balance. How can we start dealing with the way others judge us without first being on our own side?

BITESIZE BIBLE BITS

"For you formed my inward parts; you knitted me together in my mother's womb. I praise you, for I am fearfully and wonderfully made."

- Psalm 139:14 (NIV)

NIKKI'S STORY

The eldest of three girls, I was the bossy sister; but from ten years old I was bullied at school, which really knocked my confidence. I never really believed I was pretty because of my height (I hated towering over the boys and teachers at school), bushy hair and, thanks to puberty, acne. My family used to tease me about having a big nose and though they probably only meant it good humouredly, it really affected me. As a result, I walked around with my head down, desperate to blend into the background. At home, I had a good appetite but rather than this being a good thing, it was frowned upon, and I was labelled as greedy despite being very thin. Those were difficult years, but though I spent hours in my room alone reading or piano playing, I did have some good friends that I could trust and talk to. Eventually, my confidence grew enough to deal with the bullies (check out the My Friendships chapter) and my family moved to Ireland where there was a huge culture change. People there were friendlier and much more family oriented. My new friends often had at least four siblings and somehow it made them much more tolerant and, dare I say, kinder? Despite being fifteen, there was less pressure to have a boyfriend, to have sex or to take drugs than there had been in my old school and, weirdly, nobody teased me about my height or appearance! As I moved through my teens this was probably one of my happiest times, but it took a little longer for my body confidence to grow. I was still taller than many boys my age, and, desperate to fit in and not be noticed, I dressed in baggy, shapeless clothes and didn't bother too much with makeup or with haircuts (my mum trimmed my hair when it got a bit straggly). I pretended I didn't care about the way I looked.

Slowly, over the next few years, as boys appeared on the horizon, I began to emerge from my shell. Spurred on by friends, I started to take more care with my appearance. I was even persuaded to attend a modelling course. (Remember I'm very tall!) I still had acne and I was told I'd have to get rid of it if I ever wanted to model, but I was just relieved no one mentioned my nose! To deflect from the perceived ugliness of my face I started to wear clothes that accentuated my figure and I noticed that men were attracted. To me, that was positive affirmation and my skirts got shorter.

BITESIZE BIBLE BITS

"Do you not know that your bodies are temples of the Holy Spirit, who is in you, whom you have received from God? You are not your own; you were bought at a price. Therefore honour God with your bodies."

- 1 Corinthians 6:19-20 (NIV)

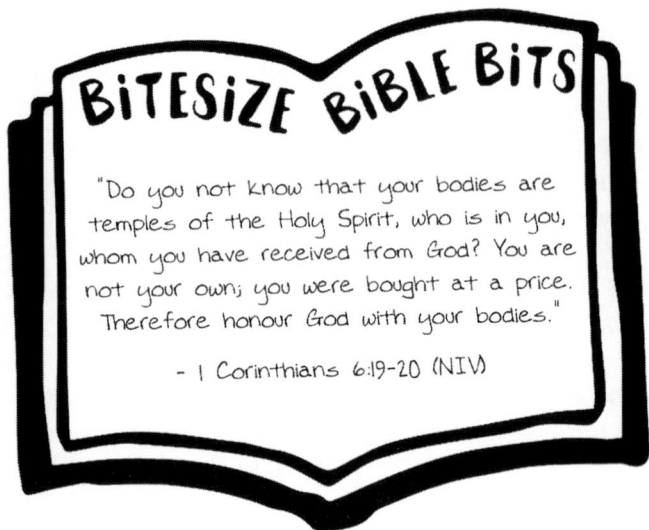

WHAT ARE YOU TELLING THE WORLD?

It's good to take care of ourselves; in fact we are told in the Bible to take care of ourselves. I quite like the story of Esther in the Bible where she spends a whole year having beauty treatments and eating special food before she was ready to be presented to the king! We have all been blessed by bodies and as long as we honour God in the treatment of our bodies, we can adorn them with beautiful art, wear cosmetics, style our hair, wear jewellery, and exercise for fitness and strength.

Throughout the ages and across the different cultures, attractiveness is measured in so many different ways. For example historically, pale skin was considered attractive when it signified that a person was so rich they didn't have to work outdoors. Then, when holidays in the sun became popular, tans became desirable. Now that we know more about sun damage, paler skin is once again becoming prized.

When we change our bodies or embellish them we need to be aware of the messages we are giving the world, and that will depend on the perceptions of the culture around us. Go back to Nikki's story for a minute. She dressed in extremely short skirts partly because she wanted to be liked by men. However, she realised in doing this, she attracted the wrong type of men, not men that would honour and respect her. When we wear provocative clothes, it could be perceived that we are sexually available, and we could get hurt in the process. Don't get us wrong, short skirts are great but whatever we choose to wear, we should wear it for ourselves, not for anyone else!

NUGGET OF TRUTH

Instead of being your best critic, try being kind to yourself. You never know, you might feel better.

WHOSE VOICE DO WE LISTEN TO, THEN?

With the prevalence of social media and 24/7 television streaming, the constant barrage of images and expectations are coming at us from all directions and our body confidence is under constant attack. It can force us to look in the wrong places and listen to the wrong voices. Often, we try to replicate the rich and famous as their perfect images relentlessly fill our eyes and our minds. Did you know that the current images portrayed in the media as the 'ideal' are actually achievable for less than 5% of the population? This is largely because those pictures are digitally enhanced, morphed and photoshopped into unrealistic images. 5% is such a tiny percentage! Yet what percentage of our thoughts are taken up with those images and aspirations?

"Four in ten teenagers said that things their friends have said have made them worry about their body image"
"Almost half of 18-25 year olds said images on social media had caused them to worry about their body image"
"One in four men have felt depressed because of concerns about their body image" (Mental Health Foundation 2019)

But, even the 5% are not necessarily body confident. Much of what society and social media teaches us about the perfect body is a lie. Most pictures have been edited, and some celebrities will not even allow a 'real' picture of themselves to be published. Remember in 2021 the controversy around the unedited photograph of Khloe Kardashian? She is someone who the world deems as 'beautiful' yet she uses Instagram filters and edits her own pictures. Why? Reading Khloe's twitter, she is a lovely, kind, generous person, yet she feels she has to maintain her perfect body image. She works incredibly hard to sustain that persona and writes about 'the pressure, constant ridicule and judgement she has endured her entire life to be perfect.' (Sean Morrison - Evening Standard April 2021).

A NOTE ON PUBERTY

Puberty means hormonal changes and new experiences beyond our control. Our bodies naturally change and grow, our weight and shape fluctuates, our skin-types change as we battle with spots and blackheads. All of these things impact our self-esteem and confidence. We all grow and develop at different rates: some of us will be embarrassed that we're developing more than our friends, while others of us are afraid we're not developing physically at all. It can be hard and can feel like an attack from all angles as we're bombarded with ideals and expectations.

CASE STUDY - ELEANOR'S STORY

My journey with body confidence began when I was around 8. I remember my sister and cousin both did gymnastics, while I played rugby and I felt as though they were much slimmer and more elegant than me. At that time I started binning things from my packed lunch at school, thinking if I were slimmer I would feel more confident and be liked more. When I was 12, I got accepted into a regional rugby team. While I was proud of this achievement, I didn't feel confident in my abilities as I felt as though I wasn't strong or fit enough, so I began doing a lot of exercise in my spare time. By 15, I was not eating and I did around 9 hours of exercise a day in an effort to make myself stronger and fitter. When I collapsed on the pitch during district trails, I was told I had to stop playing rugby. While I had been deteriorating physically, I had also been deteriorating mentally and felt I was very overweight, was obsessed with my body image and lacked confidence in every area of my life. I was diagnosed with anorexia nervosa, and admitted to hospital where I stayed for 9 months for treatment of my physical health. Anorexia treatment requires weight gain, and while this was necessary, it caused my mental health to worsen. When I was discharged from hospital, I maintained a healthy weight, but my mental health was worse than ever due to my complete lack of body confidence. I struggled with this for around 4 years, and went through stages of excessive exercise, fasting, overdoses and intensive mental health treatments. When I went on holiday 4 years after being discharged from hospital and couldn't go swimming with my younger brother, who was begging for me to go in the pool with him, I decided I had to make a conscious effort to change. I have found that for some people body confidence appears to come naturally, while others have to work harder to feel comfortable within their own skin. I'm someone who has to work harder, and there are a number of things I do every day to improve my confidence. I have found one of the most helpful things is to remind myself of what my body does for me. When I was poorly and at my lowest weight there were a lot of things I was unable to do, whereas now I maintain a healthy weight I am able to do sports, spend time travelling and exploring and work in a job I love. Another thing I have found helpful is to allow myself time for rest and relaxation without feeling guilty. While before I was focussed on improving my body physically, I now focus on improving my state of mind and mental health through doing things I enjoy, pampering myself and spending time outdoors surrounded by nature. I find this helps me appreciate the bigger picture and prevents me getting caught up in the need for the perfection of my body I previously sought. I also make a conscious effort not to compare myself to others. This is difficult, especially with social media being such a prominent part of our lives, but I find it helpful to focus on my strengths, and compare myself against these rather than other people's strengths. I compete only with the person I was yesterday, and celebrate my own achievements as well as those of others, rather than resenting the achievements of others and not celebrating my own.

It has been a long journey, and body confidence does not come overnight. Each day I have to remind myself of how far I have come, my achievements, and my goals and how I will achieve them. However, I now wake up and feel happy with how I look, but more importantly who I am as a person.

NUGGET OF TRUTH

Our bodies are truly amazing. We can carry things, build things, bake things, make things...

ACCEPT YOUR BODY

We really are 'fearfully and wonderfully made' and it is time that we started to believe this. Let's take a look at some things that might help us.

Guess what? Nobody's perfect. And, if we're all honest, nobody believes they are perfect. However, we all want to be liked and accepted and that's true for every *BODY*! Maybe we have been criticised about our appearance by someone close to us and after a while we begin to believe the criticism as the truth. The same goes when we repeatedly criticise ourselves. Harsh words (or even thoughts) about ourselves will hurt us. It will damage our self-esteem and ultimately prevent us from living a full, healthy life. We should challenge ourselves to be less of a critic and be more of a friend to ourselves.

Tell yourself what you like about yourself instead of what you don't and keep doing it until it becomes a habit.

LIKE YOUR BODY

Don't cringe, hear me out. Purposefully find things to like about your looks. Maybe you like your hair, face, or hands. What about your shape, shoulders, or legs? Even if it's just your toenails, tell yourself what you like and why. If you get stuck, ask a trusted friend what they like about your appearance. It is important that we surround ourselves with people who speak affirmation over us.

Next comes the trickier part - accept those things and DON'T argue! There IS a lot to like about you.

Now, think about what your body can do. Can you play sport, dance, walk, swim? Can you stretch, reach and jump for joy? Our bodies carry things, build things, bake things, make things and give people hugs. Spend a while thinking about all the things your body can and does do. Be amazed and be thankful.

TAKE CARE OF WHAT GOES IN YOUR BODY

It is really important to take care of our bodies too. It broke my heart a few weeks ago to hear of a lovely, bright and creative ten year old girl talk about how she didn't want her lunch because she was 'bigger' than the other girls in her class. She began taking things out of her lunchbox so she had less to eat. I personally know of at least 6 young people suffering with different eating disorders linked to deep feelings and emotions beyond their control. Our comparisons and complex feelings of uncertainty begin to build from such a young age and both overeating and undereating can lead to health complications. A good place to start is to learn more about nutritious foods and healthy portion sizes.

In this fast-paced life we seem to have lost the ability to savour our food and take our time at mealtimes. I once went on a course that spoke about 'mindfully eating' – to be honest I thought it was a bit weird. However, on reflection the point they were making is just about being present in the moment. Not rushing through the motions but noticing and enjoying the here and now.

Eating a balanced diet helps us look our best, it gives us the energy we need, and it boosts our body image. When we treat our body right, we feel good about ourselves.

TAKE CARE OF HOW YOU LOOK AFTER YOUR BODY

But it's not just about what we put in our bodies, it is also how we treat them too. Both sleep and exercise are very important. They boost our immunity, our mental wellbeing, can prevent diabetes and ward off heart disease. Being active every day doesn't necessarily mean becoming gym obsessed or that we have to attend every available workout class; in fact over-exercising can be very damaging. To be strong, fit and healthy, our bodies need to move, but we can have fun doing it.

. . .

There are some simple things we can do in order to improve our sleep. Form a regular sleep routine: turning off screens an hour or so before actually going to bed can help us to wind down, and creating a calm atmosphere will soon send us dozing into the land of nod! There are some great Apps out there that might help like Calm, Headspace, Smiling Mind, Abide to name a few.

———

Dear Lord

Help me to see myself the way you see me. Take my insecurities, self-doubts and feelings of inferiority and replace them with love, self-worth and peace. Surround me with people who lift me and love me for who I am. Show me what you love about me and help me to celebrate my body in a way that honours you. You don't make rubbish. In your eyes I am crafted to perfection and whole. I am your child. Help me to live my life in that knowledge.

Amen.

CHAPTER 2

My Fears

AS HUMAN BEINGS we have two main emotions, love and fear, from which all other emotions stem. While love is largely energy giving and positive, fear is often thought of as the evil, energy-sapping emotion. However, fear does have an important role to play in our lives. It is the innate primal response that we have to sense danger and keep us alive. It's only when we allow fear to take over and create anxiety that it can become a crippling, life-debilitating enemy. However, if managed well, fear can be good for us. It can push us to grow and expand our horizons. It can be the catapult that drives us to explore new places or situations. It can push us to revise for that exam or perform the parachute jump for charity. But (and this is a big but) fear needs to be controlled. We can't let it take over.

F.E.A.R = False Expectations Appearing Real

WHY ARE WE AFRAID? (THE TECHNICAL BIT)

Cast your mind back thousands of years ago. Early man is sitting by the fire, minding his own business and generally trying to keep warm. He hears a rustle in the trees and is instantly alert, frowning into the darkness. Is it a squirrel? A wild pig? Or is it simply the wind? He holds his breath; ears pricked, hackles raised. A twig snaps, and this time the sound appears closer. His heart beats faster; sweat beads on his forehead as he grips his club. Like a wolf, he sniffs the air, peers into the night and listens. Suddenly, with an almighty roar, a ravenous sabre-toothed tiger springs from the undergrowth intent on dinner. Pause! This is the split second in which the man has to make a decision; run or fight. Both decisions carry risk, yet the right one will potentially save his life.

Many millennia later, the fight or flight instinct is still intact. This inbuilt automatic response comes from the part of our primitive brain called the amygdala. Although our brains have significantly developed since these early human days, the amygdala is still very much alive and kicking. Like an inbuilt antenna, it sits dormant for most of the time, but as soon as it detects danger it will jump into 'live mode'. Whatever the threat, it will warn us of danger and provide us with an instinctive solution. It is like an alarm, a signal that is there to warn us to be careful. However, though this 'fear' alarm is very useful, fear also can be overwhelming and debilitating, and rather than protecting us, can cause us harm.

NUGGET OF TRUTH

If at first you don't succeed, that's actually quite normal, just try again...and again...

WHEN FEAR TURNS UGLY

There are times when fear becomes so severe that we get stuck between the fight or flight response. It's as though our bodies hit the malfunction button and we become petrified. We can't run and we can't face the fear, and whenever we experience whatever it is that makes us afraid we go into this same malfunction. It becomes a habitual fear. This type of fear is known as a phobia. Most of us know that our phobias are irrational, yet we cannot control them. Did you know 25% of all Britons suffer with acrophobia; a fear of heights? Other common phobias in the UK include glossophobia (fear of public speaking), ophidiophobia (fear of snakes), aerophobia (fear of flying) arachnophobia (fear of spiders) and agoraphobia (fear of crowds and/or of being outside). (YouGov Market Research) Phobias are very common, but they can bring on an anxiety or panic attack and a visit to the GP might be necessary to help you find the right assistance.

ANXIETY

Anxiety is a feeling of unease that can be mild (just there in the background) or severe (takes over our lives and changes the way we live). Today one in nine young people suffer from anxiety (Katherine Hill, Care for the Family). In fact, both our daughters have suffered from severe anxiety in the last few years, neither of them as a result of Covid (though this probably made it worse).

Despite both girls being very different, they equally struggled with the outside world. Neither girl could leave the house, even to take a short trip out in the car. Their worlds became very small and constrained. No amount of reassurance helped, and though to us adults the fear was irrational and made little sense, the fear was very real to them. Thankfully, both girls are working through it, and with help have overcome much of the fear they had previously. There is hope and support for people like our girls. They can beat fear.

BITESIZE BIBLE BITS

"So do not fear, for I am with you; do not be dismayed, for I am your God. I will strengthen you and help you; I will uphold you with my righteous right hand"

- Isaiah 41: 10 (NIV)

SARAH'S STORY

During sixth form, I started going out with a boy from my church. He was good looking, funny and considered quite a catch. We dated for eighteen months and my confidence soared. My status swelled and I advanced a few steps up the food chain. I felt accepted and validated. I was madly and deeply in love and nothing could pop my bubble of happiness.

And then, with a huge bang, it did. He dumped me and I was devastated. Suddenly, the fear of rejection sparked and exploded and I panicked. Remember that amygdala part of the brain mentioned earlier in this chapter? Well, boy did it kick in! Only, rather than a sabre-tooth tiger attack, it was the intense fear of being alone and unloved. My fight or flight response kicked in and I did the worst possible thing I could have done! I ran. Not away, but to my boyfriend's house, where I hammered on the door, screamed through his letterbox and sat sobbing on his doorstep – I completely and utterly made a fool of myself. Of course he ignored me and it felt like the end of the world. For months, probably even years, I pined for him. I was broken hearted and felt that no one would ever love me again.

Rejection robbed me of my confidence. It made me question who I was. Later, as I began to mend, I found comfort in the fact that Jesus knows exactly what it is like to feel rejected and found even more comfort in the fact that He will never reject us. Six months after my doorstep fiasco, I met my future husband at a friend's party. The meeting was fleeting, a brief moment when I noticed him, dancing with someone else, next to me. I thought enough of that brief encounter to mention it to my mum but thought no more of it until, four years later, I met him again in a different part of the country. God knew His plan for me, even if I didn't.

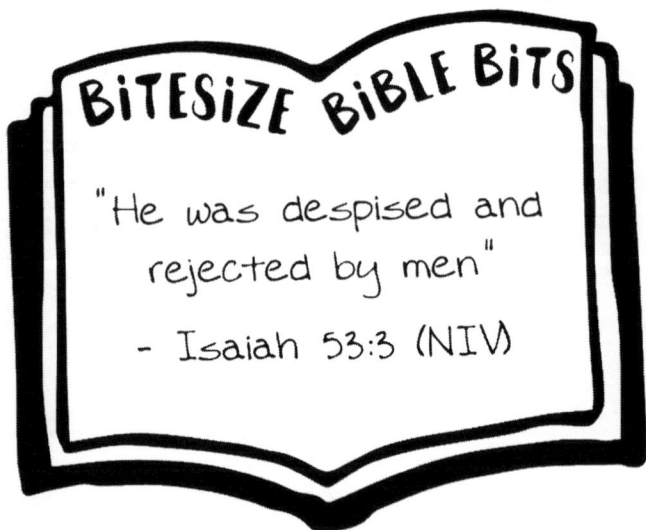

BITESIZE BIBLE BITS

"He was despised and rejected by men"

- Isaiah 53:3 (NIV)

NIKKI'S STORY

Much of my life growing up was steeped in fear. My family were a volatile lot and though sometimes I'd be praised and given the love that I craved, other times there was a lot of upset. Most of the time, being the eldest I'd do anything to keep the peace, because if anger was allowed to erupt in my household it would go on for days and would hurt. Saying and doing the right thing became necessary for survival.

I loved my mum very much. In her early life she'd been hurt badly, and this had an enormous effect on her. I knew it was important to keep her happy, and learned that if I liked the things she liked and agreed with her opinions, this would please her and she would love me. Of course, as I grew older and formed my own opinions this became more difficult, but still I tried to keep her happy. Following my exams, I received a place at Exeter University to study to become a music teacher. It was a good university and I was very excited to be going. However, my mum was devastated that I would be so far away and begged me to take an inferior place closer to home. I agreed simply to keep the peace, but unfortunately that bad decision led to many others until, following an ultimatum, I left home for good. I cut myself off, no longer able to cope with the constant fallout. I felt so far away from God, and believed he too had rejected me.

For the next few years I suffered from a real fear of not being good enough. I scraped through my degree and turned my back on teaching. I decided to only take things on if I thought I would excel. The thought of failure terrified me. However, I did very well in the business world and worked hard to move up through the ranks. I moved in with my boyfriend (who is now my husband) and was too afraid to go to church because I was 'living in sin' and worried that people would judge me. Fear consumed me in everything except my work, but eventually I came close to breaking point and cried out to God. He didn't seem to answer directly: but slowly, surrounded by good friends, including my future husband, I began to mend.

You could say in many ways I was paralysed by fear. Perhaps I should have had the courage to face my mum, because cutting myself off created much hurt on both sides. Rather than moving in with my boyfriend, which was the easiest option, perhaps I should have lived with some girlfriends and joined a church family. But I didn't, and you know what? God has still turned everything around. I am no longer so fearful and despite all my failures I know I'm a child of God.

The truth is, nothing is impossible for God. No matter how much you think you've ruined your life or have allowed fear to rule you, you are also a child of God and He can change things for you too. Believe me, I still mess up and allow fear to creep in now and again. I allow that sinister voice to mock me and tell me I can't do something, that I'll never be good enough. When that happens, before it gets too bad I force myself to look up. I remind myself God is real and He's my father. He's bigger than anything and will squish out fear in a millisecond.

BiTESiZE BiBLE BiTS

"I lift up my eyes to the mountains - where does my help come from?
My help comes from the Lord, the Maker of heaven and earth"

- Psalm 121:1-2 (NIV)

CASE STUDY - REUBEN'S STORY

Fears? I have many of them but the one that grips me the most is the fear of death. It started when I was around 10 and got progressively worse over the next few years. It wasn't a fun experience or exciting, but I have slowly learnt to manage it over time, although it still sometimes catches me unawares.

I would see things in the media or overhear things at school linked to death or people dying, and although it wouldn't immediately affect me, right before bed when my phone was off and my mind had nothing to think about, it would hit me. My thoughts would always resort back to those things I had seen or heard. I would get a nervous feeling in my stomach. Thoughts would race across my mind; *What is the point of life? What does death feel like? What is after death? If there isn't anything after, what does nothing feel like?* I would shake. My senses would heighten. I wouldn't be able to walk well. It was so hard to concentrate on anything but those fears.

I had been brought up as a Christian, going to church and believing that there is life after death – but it didn't take away those fears. I just didn't know for sure. It was as though the fear of not knowing for certain what happens when you die was worse than the actual fear itself. I was having trouble sleeping and it began to dominate my thinking more than just at nighttime. At the start of the Covid-19 pandemic it got really bad. People were talking about this virus that could kill you and my fears intensified. At first, I would just keep my thoughts and fears to myself and lie awake in bed. Then I realised that it was getting worse: it was taking over my whole thinking, and I needed some help, so I reached out to my parents and trusted adults.

I learned that when I began to get fearful, and before the climax of my panic, I could find my trusted adult and talk to them about it. Although there wasn't an immediate effect it lessened my worries quite a bit just to know that someone else knew. Another thing that I found helpful was to get two different notebooks. And when I felt I was going to start getting worried, I would write down the thing that I was worrying about in one of the books and in the other I would write three things that were good about my day and that I was grateful for. This would take my mind off the worry and help me think about things that were happy and exciting *(always do the worry first)*. Finally, what really helped was talking to my most trusted friend in my class. Although it can be a bit embar-rassing, you might find out that they had the same worry as you before and that they got through it. If they can do it, so can you. My fear has not gone away but I am learning to recognise it and manage it.

NUGGET OF TRUTH

The weakest thing you can do when you're struggling is NOT to ask for help.

UNCONDITIONAL LOVE

When fears of rejection, loneliness and failure loom large it can become overwhelming. One way to help manage these fears is to find unconditional love and acceptance. This is not an easy task; we often look for acceptance in the wrong places. Many of us find unconditional love and acceptance at home, but some of us have not had the family upbringing where stability, support and unconditional love is present. If this is the case, it is still possible to find people who can be part of your team, to be your cheerleaders: people who will listen, empathise and offer perspective. You might find your people in a church, your wider family, a club or a youth group. With unconditional love and acceptance, you can learn to take rejection in your stride and become resilient. But also never forget that God's love for you never fails, and He's your biggest champion of all.

MANAGE THOSE THOUGHTS

Most of the time, a certain amount of worry and stress is normal. It helps to keep us motivated and to get up in the morning. But sometimes, if we don't manage it correctly, it can take over. By learning a few simple techniques, we can ensure our worry stays under control.

- Write the fear down. Describe the fear and say what it is that most worries you. What are the consequences? What is the worst thing that could happen?
- Talk to a trusted person about the fear and your written thoughts above.
- Take the time to acknowledge that fear and worry are perfectly normal feelings and recognise that fears will grow bigger if we focus on them too much.

NUGGET OF TRUTH

There is nothing better than sharing your worries with a good friend and knowing they won't judge you.

SHELVE IT

Another thing that can help with fear is to visualise our fear as a little person (a bit like Morph – a plasticine character). Then say the following words aloud: "Fear, I know that you are here but I don't want to talk to you at the moment, so I am going to put you over here on this shelf until you decide to go away." Then imagine putting the little character up on a shelf. Whenever the fear threatens to control your mind, practise this and soon it will become habit. You're not ignoring the fear, you're taking control over it. Sometimes, putting the fear away up on the shelf will be easy, but other times it might be a struggle. Be patient with yourself and don't forget to celebrate your successes.

BE GRATEFUL

Being told to be grateful can grate! But the truth is that fear withers where gratitude thrives. Negative thoughts can lead to further worry and stress, but appreciation and positive thinking go a long way towards a feeling of contentment.

When we express gratitude, our brain releases dopamine and serotonin; two crucial neurotransmitters responsible for our emotions, and sometimes known as "happy chemicals". They enhance our mood immediately and make us feel good. When fear threatens, it is hard to remember to be grateful; but if you can get into the habit of being grateful it can transform your thought process. You might want to try any of the following:

- Start a daily gratitude journal
- Each day post a photo of something that makes you happy on Instagram - it might be something as simple as a mug of hot chocolate

- Make a gratitude board for your bedroom wall or have a gratitude jar where you can pop little notes inside

We have recently started a tradition of going around the table at a mealtime and sharing four things we are grateful for. At first it can be a struggle to find any positives but the more we practise it, the more we notice the tiny things. It's not uncommon for one of us to say "I'm grateful for my comfortable bed," or "I'm grateful the bus arrived on time this morning." It sounds silly but I promise you, it really does work!

BITESIZE BIBLE BITS

"For God has not given us a spirit of fear and timidity, but of power, love and of self-discipline."

- 2 Timothy 1:7 (NLT)

FINALLY

Fear is real but you can take control of it before it controls you. Look around you and notice the beauty that surrounds you. Be fully present in the moment and aware of the good things in your life. Find people that love and accept you unconditionally, and never forget your Heavenly Father is there - even when it doesn't feel as though He is.

———

Dear Lord

In your word you tell me that if I place all my fears, worries and burdens into your hands, You will give me peace. Please help me to do this and not take them back. You have given me a sound mind, a mind that I can control. Please give me wisdom, fill my heart with your goodness and remind me of all the wonderful things there are in life if I look for them. Help me to fix my thoughts on what is true, honourable, right, pure and lovely, and guide me towards the purpose and plan you have for me. Surround me with people who love me without conditions or judgement. Thank you that above all, You love and accept me no matter what mistakes and bad decisions I make.

Amen

CHAPTER 3

My Mental Health

BACK WHEN OUR grandparents and great-grandparents were young, mental illness was something you never talked about. It certainly existed, but lack of knowledge and understanding meant that people were afraid of it and pretended it wasn't there. During the first world war (1914 – 1918), thousands of young men suffered from what was then known as shell shock following their experiences in the trenches. Doctors put it down to exploding shells damaging the brain until they learned that not all of the men experienced the shells, but all were experiencing the same symptoms: terrifying dreams, loss of memory, insomnia, emotional instability, lack of self-control and more. At first, these poor men were called cowards and sent back to the front. It wasn't until much later that medical professionals agreed the soldiers were suffering from a real mental illness (in this case Post-Traumatic Stress Disorder) which needed professional treatment.

Thankfully, today we are a lot more understanding; the truth is that many people suffer with mental disorders, and in all probability most of us will suffer at some time. In 2020 16% of children aged between 5 and 16 were diagnosed with probable mental disorder compared with 10.8% in 2017 (www.digital-NHS.co.uk). Covid definitely played a part in this as young people were cut off from friends, school, and wider family as well as being exposed to hours of media coverage about death and threat of sickness. It was as though the whole world had gone into hiding and everyone felt helpless. Parents voiced their concerns and children couldn't help but listen, which caused further worry and anxiety.

Traditionally, when we talk about health we tend to think about our physical health and fitness. Most of us agree (especially as we get older) we can't take our physical health for granted. The same has to be said about our mental health.

NUGGET OF TRUTH

We can't take our mental health for granted. Just like our physical health, it needs care and exercise.

NIKKI'S STORY

"Leave your boyfriend or leave home!" That was the ultimatum. So I left home with two bin bags filled with clothes and a guitar. I took a taxi to my student boyfriend's digs, sobbing all the way, not really sure if I'd made the right decision. I'd rung a trusted friend and a family member to ask their advice and they both agreed leaving home was probably best. Probably. Worse, I couldn't believe my mum would let me go like that.

A year passed and to the outside world, I was doing well. I had a part time job, was studying to be a teacher and engaged to be married. But then, without warning, I hit rock bottom. It was as if the gravity of my actions and my mother's rejection crashed into me and my world collapsed. Suddenly, I was unable to leave the house. I'd pack my stuff ready for lectures, open the front door and couldn't take one step outside. I really couldn't. Then, uncontrollable tears came and wouldn't stop flowing. I didn't want to see or speak to anyone. I'd picked at my hair so badly, there was a mass of short ends sticking out of the side of my head. I didn't realise it then, but I now know I wasn't well. My fiancée took me to see the doctor who diagnosed exhaustion and prescribed me with a course of Valium. I literally slept solidly for two weeks and then over the next few years with professional therapy and support, I gradually got better. Back then no one really mentioned mental disorder; today, I know I had experienced some sort of mental breakdown.

―――――

TEEN MENTAL HEALTH

Mental health is about how we think, feel and act. Sometimes we feel well, and sometimes we don't. When our mental health is good, we feel motivated and able to take on challenges and new experiences. But when our mental health is not so good, we can find it much harder to cope. Like our physical health, we can often take our mental health for granted until something knocks us off our feet and causes us to struggle. Often, we don't see it coming. According to statistics, three quarters of mental illnesses are first experienced before the age of 20, so it is something we can't ignore. Recently, a prominent professor commented:

"We've seen deteriorations in mental health broadly over the last couple of decades. We've seen an upward shift in depression, anxiety, self-harm... Children and young people are falling through the cracks in terms of service provision."

(Yvonne Kelly, Professor of Lifecourse Epidemiology and Public Health at University College London)

Adolescence can be a tricky time. Our bodies are changing and our thoughts and personalities are developing. We are learning more about who we are, forming our ideas and beliefs, and developing our characters. We can sense that our independence is growing, and our choices are becoming our own. But at the same time, we can feel terrified and even debilitated. Pressures of comparisons and competing can be overwhelming. This should be an exciting time in our lives but it can also crush us. The mental health we may have taken for granted is suddenly put to the test, and before we have time to realise it, we can spiral out of control. Desperate for release, we turn to harmful behaviours and make unwise choices which impact both our mental and physical health.

NUGGET OF TRUTH

Sometimes life can feel like we're wading through syrup, but with the right recipe of care we'll make it to the waffle!

SARAH'S STORY

Many members of my family, at different points of their lives, have battled with anxiety, a battle that is never entirely won. I don't know whether you have had experience of anxiety or not, but for me it appears to slowly sneak up and, like a stalker, follows me from a distance until one day, my walk becomes tough and the shadows catch up with me. Anxiety is right there and I can't seem to shake it off.

When my daughter was born, she looked like a perfect doll. She seemed to 'know' things right from the start. It was as though she analysed every situation and every person. She loved to be creative, to make things and to write and draw. She was reading well before school and could write her name and form most letters by the age of three.

She was good at many things, gifted you might say, but she always struggled with play. I would take her to play groups and she would just want to sit with me. I would go to friends' houses with children of a similar age, and she would be very happy sitting with the adults while the other children played. Her school target in reception class was to leave the writing table and go and play with others. She would often stay silent when people asked her questions, and I quickly got into the habit of answering for her.

As she grew older, she succeeded in school. People praised her for her writing ability and artwork, for her sensible and helpful behaviour and her reliability. As her mum, I took this for granted. Yes, she might be quiet in social situations, but academically, she was thriving and everyone thought very highly of her.

It wasn't until secondary school that her insecurities took hold and life suddenly became very difficult for her. That confidence she seemingly once had, disappeared overnight and we were left with a shell of our once creative and energised daughter. Whether it was the change of school, the pressure of new friends, teachers' expectations or the ever-increasing hormones we didn't know, but we knew we could no longer take her mental health for granted. It was so painful to watch her suffer, shrouded by fear, anxiety and pure mental exhaustion. At night I sat with her through panic attacks, I watched her struggle to eat due to the knots in her stomach and I cried when I saw the scars on her body where she had self-harmed. I knew that in her worst moments she had thought about taking her own life and knew how she might do it. I felt utterly helpless and it almost broke me. It was in those dark moments that I dug deep and held onto my ounce of faith that there was a God out there who loved her, who had a plan for her and was sitting with her in her anguish.

CASE STUDY - HARRIET'S STORY

Reading what my mum has written about me really hit me hard. Finally seeing it from the outside and how bad it really did get at points breaks my heart now. I feel for the girl who couldn't sleep or eat or leave the house or see her friends or get through a day at school.

It is so draining, constantly being on high alert and over-thinking everything; dealing with the physical symptoms all day everyday exhausted me. It left me with little to no energy or mental capacity to even think about doing or going anywhere 'fun'. It took so much just to get through the day. I felt, and still sometimes feel, like I have failed as a person, a friend, a girlfriend, a child, a sister, an employee and failed myself for not being able to do things like other people. But needing help, extra support, time out, explanations and saying no to things does not make you a burden.

As well as affecting my mental wellness, it also led me to physically harming myself. I can't pinpoint exactly why it became such a coping mechanism; however I think that it is definitely a scarily common one. I felt trapped in my body and in my head and it was almost like a release, proving I am real and taking my attention away from the mental pain to the physical pain. As a bit of a cry for help, I wanted people to understand the extent of how I was feeling because it was so hard to explain.

I also cannot pinpoint exactly how I began to reduce self-harming and anxious intrusive thoughts, it just kind of happened. I eventually came to realise of my own accord that it was neither a productive nor a healthy coping mechanism. I didn't like the version of me that self-harmed and I didn't want to keep having to hide parts of my body. There is nothing to be ashamed of about self-harm scars but I knew I needed to tell someone and get some help before it got completely out of control.

One of the super simple things that I find works a lot of the time now is distraction; simply waiting for a bit of time to pass rather than acting on the impulse when the emotions of the triggering event/thought are high. Now, I know what you are all thinking.. "Distraction! That's what everyone says!" And to be honest I agree with you, distracting yourself especially when the anxiety feels all-encompassing is wayyyyy easier said than done! However, I can assure you that it becomes easier with practice. I have learnt over the past few years that even silly little things like dancing or even stomping around in your room genuinely makes a difference - maybe blasting your favourite music. You are releasing the pent up energy and urges in a safe and healthy way, waiting for some time to pass and hopefully the feelings to subside.

I think it is also important to remember that healing is most definitely not linear. I have had many ups and downs, more positive times and relapses over the years. I don't know one person who felt better overnight and never felt bad again - that's just not realistic. Especially in the church, you do hear stories of people praying then being 'cured' overnight and that's amazing, I'm happy they got to experience that but just because that might not be the case for you or others, doesn't mean you are unworthy or unloved by God.

The last thing I want to touch on is gratitude - it is something that has really helped me. Romanticising and taking a moment to appreciate the little things in each day. For example, the sunset, the taste of your favourite chocolate, a smile you received or gave someone or even just that you survived the day! Journaling and writing these small things down is something I have been trying to do more often so that could be something that helps you too? Maybe give it a try for a week or so and see what happens! These things really do add up when you start to practice the act of gratitude and you will begin to see, even without realising, that life is worth living - it is beautiful and so are you!

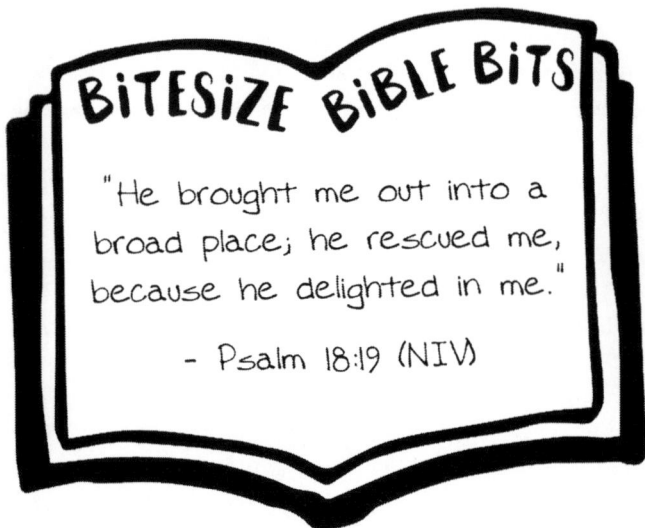

BITESIZE BIBLE BITS

"He brought me out into a broad place; he rescued me, because he delighted in me."

- Psalm 18:19 (NIV)

THERE IS HOPE

When it comes to what we can do to look after our mental health, little things help a lot. There have been times over my life when my mental health has not been at all good and I have needed to pause, re-evaluate and to find ways to move forward; but this is not easy. In his Sunday Times best seller book *S.U.M.O*, Paul McGee (www.thesumoguy.com) introduced me to the concept of 'It's ok not to be ok'. Life is not a straight road, it is more like a rollercoaster with thrills, twists, and turns. In all our lives we will meet situations or experiences that knock us, and it is necessary to press pause and take time. He goes on to say that the important thing is to remember that the 'pause' is a detour not the destination. This has really helped me, and I know it has helped many others too. It is easy to believe that when life gets tough and our mental health has taken a hit, this is the narrative of our story, the end of our journey. It isn't: it's only a season. Having worked with many young people and adults who've experienced poor mental health, I can promise you that your health doesn't need to define you. When our mental health is suffering, we need to somehow dig deep and understand there is more to us than this moment.

We have gathered some simple suggestions below that can be incorporated into our life journey. They can bring joy, calm, encouragement and ultimately build our confidence as we walk through these detours.

———

GET ACTIVE

This can feel like the last thing we want to do, but it is so important for both our physical and mental health. Regular exercise can improve our mood and self-confidence, increase our energy and help us sleep better. Start small like a short walk or choosing the stairs instead of the lift and build it up slowly. Sometimes getting active with others helps to motivate and make us accountable. Join a sports club, go swimming with a friend or just go for a stroll together. Whatever you choose to do, just making a start will make a difference - we promise!

DO SOMETHING FOR ENJOYMENT

When our mental health is really suffering, it is hard to see good or feel satisfaction in anything. We can lose our love of life, and the word fun no longer holds any meaning for us. I found a tip in Paul McGee's book *S.U.M.O* which I use for my family. When any of us feel negative about something we take a magnifying glass and place it over the positive things, no matter how small these might be. We all know that looking at something through a magnifying glass makes it appear bigger. If we focus on the negative stuff, the things that are going wrong will appear much greater than they actually are and make us feel worse. However, if we move our magnifying glass to anything remotely good (even tiny) that too will appear bigger and will immediately affect our mood.

Focusing on the things that make you happy and spending time doing activities you enjoy will improve your mood and relax you. Whatever you enjoy doing, whether it's sport, baking, spending time with friends, gaming or reading, no matter how much your mind is screaming out against it, do it anyway and focus on those tiny seeds of joy. Eventually they will grow.

LEARN TO RELAX

Relaxation in our family didn't come naturally. There was an almost inbuilt guilt if we were caught 'doing nothing.' I grew up with this mentality that I had to be always doing something, almost to validate my identity. I have had to learn to recognise that there are times for *doing* and there are times for *being*.

Focusing on being present in the moment is a skill that needs to be practised. It's about noticing the now. Working hard, keeping busy and achieving in school, exams and jobs are all important, but none of these things define us. We need to learn that just being us is enough. Slow down, take out some time to clear your mind and feel peaceful and calm. Spend time in nature, read, listen to music, have a bath, meditate, or perhaps pray. All of these things will relax you and bring you a sense of calm.

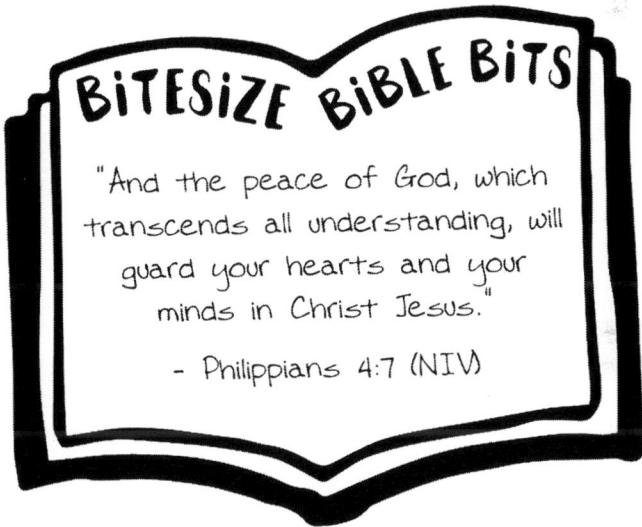

BITESIZE BIBLE BITS

"And the peace of God, which transcends all understanding, will guard your hearts and your minds in Christ Jesus."

- Philippians 4:7 (NIV)

These are just a few small exercises you can try if you feel overwhelmed. However, mental wellbeing is a serious matter, and if things start to feel they're getting out of hand - for example, if you cannot leave the house or are tempted to turn to potentially harmful options in order to cope - please reach out for help. Ideally you could turn to your pastor, a trusted teacher or family member, but if you feel you have no one, www.kooth.com is a good place to start. Kooth is an online mental wellbeing community where you can communicate online with counsellors and emotional wellbeing practitioners. You can login anonymously, read about other people's experiences, post on forums and speak to counsellors. This site is moderated and is safe to use. Kooth also works in partnership with schools and universities and is committed to helping young people with their mental health. At the back of this book you will also find a comprehensive list of agencies and charities that may help.

―――――

YOU ARE LOVED

Even if you do have a faith in God, you may sometimes feel that He is absent; especially if you have been hurt by well-meaning Christians who tell you that all you need to do is pray and God will take the problem away. When God doesn't immediately take the problem away, this can make you feel unworthy and shameful for still struggling. It can seem as though God has not answered your prayer because you are not good enough or you don't have enough faith. Sometimes these well-meaning people can make you feel worse and more alone.

We want you to know that you are LOVED and you are VALUED and there is nothing you can do to change that. You can be confident that God made you, and no matter what you are going through right now, the struggles and the heartache do not define you, they shape you. You will get through this.

NUGGET OF TRUTH

No matter what our battles are,
God simply delights in us.

Dear Lord,

During these tough times, help me to hear your voice and feel
Your presence. You warned me that life would not be easy, but
promised that You will not leave me. In the Psalms when
David cried out from the depths of despair, you heard him.
Hear me too, lead me out of this darkness and help me to walk
in your ways. Your ways are healthy and nutritious for my
soul and I know that your love for me is relentless and
unconditional.

Amen

CHAPTER 4
My Mistakes

YOU WILL MAKE MISTAKES. We all do. In fact you've probably made quite a few already, and if you hadn't we'd be wondering why. Mistakes are a fact of life: it's how we learn, and if you're anything like us, no matter what our parents tell us, we think we know best, even now! We have to try things our way, so we make lots of mistakes. Even at work when more experienced colleagues give us advice, we often choose to ignore it to our detriment!

However, it can become a problem if we repeat the same mistake over again; and some mistakes can become life-long regrets if we don't correct them. If you ever get the chance to spend time in a care home for the elderly, have a chat with some of the residents. You may be lucky enough to learn about their life experiences and gain little nuggets of wisdom.

Did you know some of the most common regrets for the elderly are as follows:

1. I wish I'd travelled when I had the chance
2. I wish I'd not stayed in that relationship for so long
3. I wish I'd spent more time with my family and children. I worked too much.
4. I wish I'd taken more risks and not worried so much
5. I wish I'd had more confidence in myself as a youngster. I missed out on so many opportunities because I didn't think I was good enough
6. I wish I'd told the people important to me that I loved them.

Yes, making mistakes is important but correcting them and learning from them is even more important!

NUGGET OF TRUTH

All the great people in history made mistakes before they achieved success. And if you don't know what they were, it's because mistakes are easily forgotten.

SARAH'S STORY

Sometimes a mistake can feel so big, it feels irreversible and irreparable. When I was sixteen I had one of those experiences. I'd been having a really bad day. I can't even remember what it was about, but I do recall feeling pretty down. My confidence was at a low, I felt worthless and struggled to understand my place in the world. In order to cheer me up, my friend suggested that I take her car for a drive.

The fact that I didn't even have my learner driver's licence meant nothing to me. At that moment my brain didn't process any of the 'ifs' or 'buts', it simply loved the idea. I jumped into the driver's seat, put on my seatbelt (at least I thought of that!) and turned on the engine. I had no clue what I was doing, but it couldn't be that difficult! Everyone can drive, can't they? I listened carefully to my friend who gave me the instructions. Put your foot down on the clutch, put the gear into reverse and press down on the accelerator! Easy. My foot went on the clutch, I pushed the gear into reverse, jammed my right foot on the accelerator and lifted my left foot from the clutch. We shot backwards like a scud missile from its launcher, across the deserted road and into the neighbour's wall behind us.

Thankfully, only my pride was hurt, though we both felt a little shaken. It wasn't until we tumbled out of the car that the full impact of what I'd done hit me. My friend's car was a write off, and so was my neighbour's wall. The fact my neighbour's cat had only moments before been sunning itself on the said wall, well… let's not go there. Luckily cats have nine lives. What on earth had I been thinking?

· · ·

The truth is, I hadn't been thinking at all. I'd been caught up in the moment. I needed something to boost my self-esteem, to make me look brave in front of my friend, something exciting to give me confidence. It's just that this something backfired. Literally! A year later, I was still paying towards the new car my parents had to buy for my friend, as well as for the wall repairs. I missed out on so much, because I had lost all my savings and any future pocket money and earnings were instantly gone. However, that mistake has always stuck with me, and I learned that driving a car requires skills and must be taken seriously!

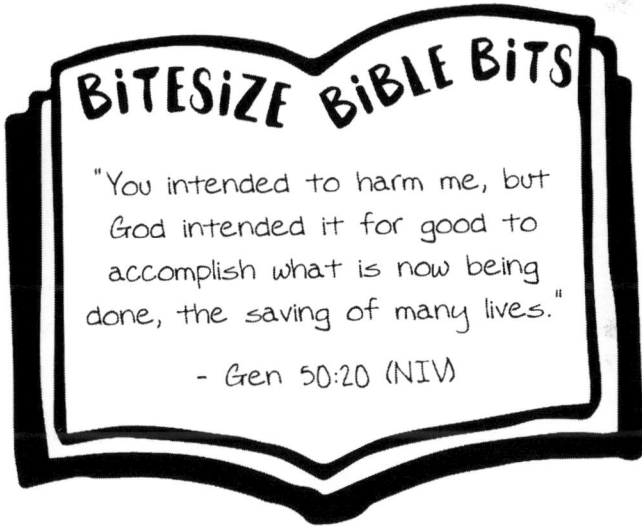

BITESIZE BIBLE BITS

"You intended to harm me, but God intended it for good to accomplish what is now being done, the saving of many lives."

- Gen 50:20 (NIV)

WHY DO WE MESS UP?

Did you know that our brains are already about 90-95% adult size by the time we're six years old? But although the brain is physically almost fully grown, it does most of its developing and extensive remodelling during puberty. The connections between different parts of our brain are strengthened and increased, or (if they're no longer needed) they are pruned away. This reconstruction process continues until our mid-twenties, so no wonder life can be a bit overwhelming and confusing at times! Our brain is made up of lots of different parts that all have specific jobs:

- Frontal lobe – thinking, planning, decision making, reasoning, judgement, movement, behaviour
- Temporal lobe – speech, hearing, learning, emotions
- Parietal lobe – language and touch
- Occipital lobe – visual processing
- Cerebellum – balance, coordination
- Brain stem – breathing, heart rate and temperature

Now, our brains develop from the back to the front. So, guess which part of the brain is the last part to develop? Yep, the frontal lobe! The bit of our brain that does the thinking, processing and reasoning. The bit that controls our behaviour. OK, now I feel a bit better about that driving mistake! You see, before our frontal lobe is fully developed, we make many of our decisions based on feelings rather than thinking them through.

―――――

NO TWO BRAINS ARE THE SAME

Everyone develops at different rates, so your brain re-modelling may be at a different stage to somebody else's. This is normal, and although our teenage years are often ones of comparison, it is important that we remember each of us is unique. During this brain re-modelling, we may find that we take more risks, feel strong emotions, make impulsive decisions, are more vulnerable to stress factors and feel tired or down at different times. It is important that we remember to be kind to ourselves and to each other – this is not an easy time! Remember: you are not alone. Talk to a trusted friend if it gets too much!

NUGGET OF TRUTH

We won't accomplish much in life if we don't take calculated risks.

NIKKI'S STORY

Like everyone else, I've made hundreds of mistakes in my life; but I want to talk about something that knocked my confidence for years, and it wasn't even that much of a bad mistake! When I was fourteen, secondary school was not my favourite place; my days were spent avoiding the intimidating, popular kids, the mean bullies and the sarcastic teachers with their acerbic tongues. Every school has them: the teacher who seems to enjoy the power they wield on the less confident kids. In my experience, it was usually the PE teachers, but we also had one in the biology department. I was pretty scared of Miss Monroe; an elderly spinster who dressed in black, knew her subject well, frowned upon those who struggled and could kill all who dared to disrupt her lesson with flashing eyes. Yes, I was terrified of Miss Monroe and wouldn't have been surprised if she hated garlic and slept in a tomb. It was a Monday morning after a particularly busy weekend, and though I'd rushed my homework on 'animal cells', I felt quite confident about it. As we marked our own work, Miss Monroe asked for answers and I tentatively put up my hand.

"Yes?" she demanded with a sneer.

"Rectum," I replied and the whole class erupted into laughter. That is, everyone except for Miss Monroe. She immediately made me stand up and asked me to explain why I would think the rectum would be part of a cell.

"Reticulum!" she roared and proceeded to call me a "stupid child!"

That moment of ridicule curbed my confidence for many years and from then on, I kept quiet! It was only when I realised my answer was often correct and I wasn't stupider than everyone else that I began to lift my hand again.

Have you ever lost your confidence as a result of a silly error? Don't make the same mistake I did and let it rob you of opportunities. Think of the number of times I didn't speak up during a class debate, give my opinion when asked or volunteer for something I would have loved to be a part of. The only person who lost was me!

HOW CAN I MOVE ON?

Our mistakes can incur financial cost (like Sarah's friend's car) but they can also be costly physically, emotionally and mentally. It's often these mistakes that take their toll on us. Moving on from them can seem impossible, but there is hope. Sometimes our mistakes will leave us with lasting scars both inside and out, but wherever you are in your relationship with God or the Christian faith, we want you to know that God sees your mistakes and He knows that they don't define you, they refine you.

If we allow Him to, God will find a way to use the results of our mistakes as a foundation on which to build new life and grow opportunities. Our scars from self-harm, our police record, our lies and damaging behaviour, our weak moments, our written-off cars – nothing is too much. All these things can be used to build from. We can learn from our pain and develop a strength that wouldn't have been possible without the discomfort. Through our messes we gain wisdom, understanding, empathy, hope and truth. Through our wrong choices we discover new ways to grow. If we let Him, God uses our mistakes for our good; to refine us and protect us. A problem can either be a catalyst for growth or it can stunt us. It is up to us how we respond.

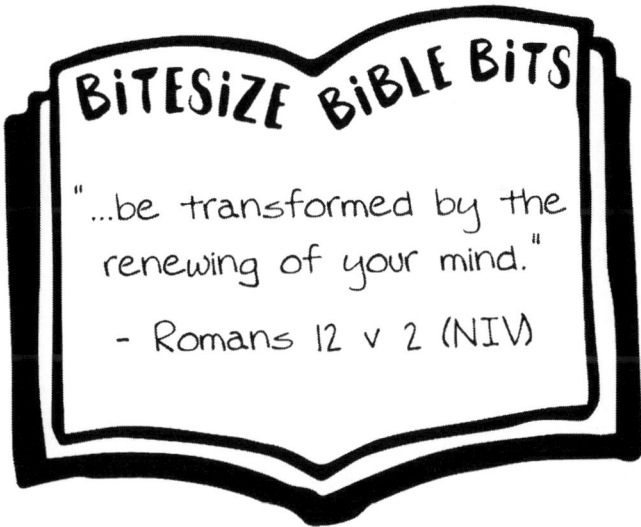

BITESIZE BIBLE BITS

"...be transformed by the renewing of your mind."

- Romans 12 v 2 (NIV)

CASE STUDY – LYDIA'S STORY

As a child I had an active imagination: teachers told me I was great at writing stories. I was a good girl, keen to 'do the right thing.'

I don't know how my anxiety started, but growing up, memories became important to me. I tried to store them all up to remember people or places I loved. The effort of remembering so much started to take its toll and my mind felt full. My active imagination was in overdrive & creating stories that weren't fun anymore. Horrid thoughts of me doing disgusting things would pop into my head for no reason, like remembering a nightmare the next day...but this nightmare wouldn't stop.

In secondary school these thoughts happened so often I couldn't count them. I felt dirty and shameful and found myself trying to 'cancel thoughts out' by repeating an action over and over until my thoughts lined up. It could take an hour to get dressed in the morning. I was trying so hard to control my mind, but an anxiety disorder called OCD was in control of me. Life was miserable. My brain felt like Christmas lights so messed up you'd be better throwing them away. I just wanted to feel 'normal.'

My mind scared me so badly I'd have regular panic attacks, sobbing until my eyes stung. I couldn't see a way out and just wanted it to stop. OCD had a hold on my life until my twenties...I saw therapists and tried medication, though a turning point came when my family moved to Lincoln and a new church. I met people who accepted me and learned that God loved me and had great plans for my life; that I'd always been good enough.

I prayed, 'God, I'm a mess, I can't live like this any longer, please help me and take this all away.' It wasn't an overnight transformation; patterns of thinking take time to re-wire themselves and getting better was a long process for me. The brain is like a muscle you can train, and over time I transformed my mind with medication, therapy, and faith. I'm grateful to those doctors who helped me, but the biggest difference was knowing God was in it with me and wouldn't leave.

Now that I'm an adult, do I still struggle with some anxiety? Yes, and it may always be something I need to deal with. But it's not my identity any more: that comes from who I am in God. That faith gave me hope my life could be better, and I believe that hope is there for you too.

––––––

THERE IS ALWAYS A WAY THROUGH

Sometimes our mistakes make us feel there is no turning back. We feel hopeless and stuck. Carol Dweck, a researcher at Stanford University, is well-known for her work on mindsets and the difference between a fixed and growth mindset.

Having a fixed mindset means that we believe *we can't, we won't,* or *we will never*. The more we and others reinforce this message into our brain, we get stuck and imagine there is no way back from our mistakes. The future is hopeless. However, the truth is that our brain is malleable and, just like any muscle in our body, we can train it so it is strengthened and more flexible. Then, we will begin to see solutions and hope. People with a growth mindset learn from mistakes and find ways to overcome challenges. They find inspiration from others who've had similar experiences. Our minds are powerful, and the stories we believe about ourselves will either drive us forward or hold us back.

• • •

A Horrible Experiment From The 1950's That We Can Learn From – Thank You Little Ratty Friends

In the 1950's, a scientist called Dr Richter did a series of experiments to test to see how long two sets of rats could survive in a high-sided bucket of water (please do not try this at home). The first group of rats could swim for about 15 minutes before giving up and sinking. With the second group of rats, Dr Richter took them out of the water just before they gave up, dried them off and gave them a brief rest before putting them back. This second group of rats could swim for an average of 60 hours! The doctor discovered that if the rat was temporarily saved and allowed to rest, it would survive 240 times longer than the first group.

What has this all got to do with our mistakes? These rats were able to survive longer because they were given hope. They knew if they swam long enough, they would be rescued and given a break. This hope gave them the energy to keep swimming. Sometimes we can be like the first group of rats, and feel that our situation or mistake is hopeless. We just want to give up. God gives us the hope to keep swimming. The hope that our mistakes can be used for good. The hope that whatever mess we have made, it is not the end.

NUGGET OF TRUTH

When you make a mistake, celebrate - you're on your way to success.

BIBLICAL FAILURES

Contrary to popular belief, the Bible is not a book of brow beatings and rules. It is a book full of stories about people who failed repeatedly, who did terrible things only to find forgiveness and love. David (the chap who defeated the giant and wrote all of those amazing psalms) not only used his power to commit adultery, he also murdered a man in cold blood so he could have his wife. Lot's daughters got their father drunk and slept with him; Sarah, Abraham's wife, couldn't get pregnant and was cruel to her fertile servant; Paul murdered hundreds of Christians before becoming a Christian himself; Peter made false promises and betrayed his dearest friend, and Matthew cheated lots of people out of their hard-earned cash.

These are just a few biblical examples of people who went through dark times. Yet none of their mistakes defined them. God did not stop loving them. God did not stop forgiving them. He used them for good. Jesus spent most of his time with people who made lots of mistakes. In contrast, he got quite cross with the church elders and Pharisees who were seemingly blameless and righteous. Be encouraged.

———

Dear Lord

Thank you that no matter what mistakes I make in my life, there is nothing that can separate Your love from me. Thank you for carrying me through the dark times, refining me and shaping me as we journey through life together. Give me the wisdom to make the right decisions but the ability to forgive myself as You forgive me over and over again.

Amen.

CHAPTER 5

My Abilities

OUR BRITISH CULTURE often teaches us to play down our abilities, that anything other than being humble about our capabilities is showing off. Yet our American friends have a completely different attitude. If complimented they will receive it openly and with pride. Maybe we should be a bit more like that. We have enough to contend with in life (quite frankly if we didn't, this book wouldn't need to exist) and perhaps we should learn to receive compliments graciously. Not only that, but compliments really do not occur very regularly. Social and cultural media tells us that to survive we must be strong and to be strong we must look after ourselves: pamper ourselves, treat ourselves, protect ourselves and so on. So, in a nutshell, we live in this funny contrast of being self-reliant and self-effacing.

Add to this the thousands of social media personalities that showcase the best moments of their lives: perfect wardrobe, perfect job, perfect friends, perfect holidays, perfect family. We have a friend who lives a perfect 'pretend' life online. She dresses up a small part of her room and makes it look fabulous, photographs it and posts it. Her followers see this magazine worthy home with fabulous design and expensive furniture. You don't get to see the true picture; the table covered with felt tip pen, the worn, comfy family sofa complete with dog hair. People see her flawless images and feel that somehow they've failed and their own house should look like this, and yet it's all a big lie! So, we are taught to underplay our abilities, overplay our self-assurance and pretend to have it all sorted. No wonder we struggle so much!

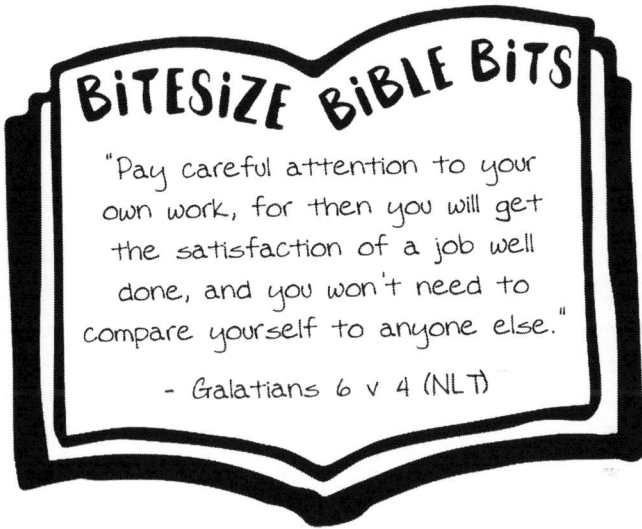

BITESIZE BIBLE BITS

"Pay careful attention to your own work, for then you will get the satisfaction of a job well done, and you won't need to compare yourself to anyone else."

- Galatians 6 v 4 (NLT)

We love this verse because it simply tells us to focus on our own journey. So many of us seem to spend too much time worrying about the abilities of others and forget to focus on developing our own skills. Rather than comparing ourselves with others and feeling inferior, perhaps we should focus on honing our skills and abilities. Let's motivate ourselves to improve and make progress, and try to see mistakes, not as failures, but as an opportunity to develop and discover new ways to move forward. This is what the verse in Galatians is all about – if we pay attention to our own work (skills, abilities, gifts, qualities) then we will feel satisfied and will have no need for comparison. However, it is not always easy and many of us fall into the trap of comparison.

———

SARAH'S STORY

Comparison is real, it can be debilitating and I'm a sucker for it.

From an early age I compared myself to others, judging myself against other's abilities, looks and attributes. For me, school sports days were filled with dread and fear. I was considered 'sporty', but each year I stood on that starting line with my heart pumping, palms sweating and knees knocking, terrified of failure and ridicule. All eyes were on me, boring into my back, expectations high.

One particularly disastrous year, I remember glancing to my left at the school cross country champion and being aware of the prettiest girl in my year on my right. I swallowed down a feeling of inadequacy and attempted to focus on the finishing line. There was anticipation in the air, and for a split second it was as though the world paused and time stood still. The whistle blew, feet began to thunder down the track, the crowds cheered and I… fell flat on my face – humiliation!

The thing is, comparing myself with others robbed me from the joy of the moment and the joy of being me. Even before I started the race, I had already allowed my thoughts to tell me I wasn't good enough and I wasn't going to win. I convinced myself that this mattered – despite knowing that running wasn't my thing. I was good at hockey, netball and a great asset in rounders, but in that moment those strengths didn't matter – I couldn't run and the girls either side of me could. Those thoughts immediately affected my confidence and that ultimately caused my downfall – quite literally in this case!

I guess I am not alone in my tendency to compare with others even when the comparison doesn't really matter.

For me, my lack of ability has often led to great fear – fear of not being worthy, fear of not being good enough, fear of not being nice enough or clever enough or pretty enough. Fear of everyone else being better than me. It is so easy to fall into that trap of fear. How about you? For some, comparing our abilities will cause a lack of confidence, for others it will cause us to retreat, for still others it means self-deprecation and self-loathing, depression, anxiety – or a cocktail of them all.

But the truth is, that cross-country champion on my left – she didn't wake up one morning, automatically a champion. No, she trained and she trained a lot. She attended cross country club practice before school in all weathers, she ran with her dad after school and went to evening running club. She had passion, skill and commitment, and she worked hard at it. Of course, I wasn't going to beat her in a school race – I didn't even like running – and that was ok. I had my own race to run, my own 'thing' to find and my own interests to pursue. A God-given, specifically created purpose – just for me! And so have you.

NUGGET OF TRUTH

When you constantly compare
with others, you will constantly
be disappointed.

GOD GIVEN ABILITIES

Think back to an art lesson when you were younger. You're asked to draw something, let's say, a dog. You draw a dog and you like your dog. Then you look at your neighbour's dog and the boy across the table's dog and the teacher's dog – and what do you do? – you compare. Now, you look back at your dog and you realise it is not as good as everyone else's. Your dog is rubbish, so why bother trying?

If you were the teacher, what would you advise that child to do? Perhaps you would praise their picture and encourage them. If you gave hints for improvement, you would make sure that they suited the child's own skills and ability.

Comparing ourselves with others will always leave us lacking. God asks us not to look at others for affirmation but to look to Him, and He thinks we are pretty terrific!

You have skills, abilities and gifts that are unique to you. Perhaps you know what they are already. Maybe they're in their infancy, or you may still be in that place of searching and discovering them. We have a lifetime of discovery.

It is so easy to focus our searching on observing the

achievements and abilities of those around us. This is natural and normal, but if we spend time looking at our own nature, character and interests, and focus on what God says about us, then we will be able to discover and develop our own abilities. The ones chosen for us. The ones to build our self-esteem, perseverance and feeling of pride. The ones to work on to develop, hone and grow. The ones that are worth stepping out of our comfort zone for and pursuing. Each of us is unique. God made us that way. So, let's stop looking to our right and to our left. Let us instead look in and up and see what wonders we discover.

NUGGET OF TRUTH

Life is not a dress rehearsal, live it now.

NIKKI'S STORY

I left college with low self-esteem. I had no idea what I wanted to be or what I wanted to do; I only knew I'd had enough of the education system. Despite having little confidence in my own ability, I was determined to prove the world wrong: I could make my own way in the world and I didn't need anyone to help me do it! I washed my hands of my family and condescending tutors, bought a suit and landed myself a temporary job through an admin agency. It wasn't easy. Fresh out of college, I was naïve and had to learn quickly, and everyone wanted to know why I didn't immediately go on to become a teacher. Was I lazy? A drop-out? However, I wasn't a stranger to hard work, since I'd worked my way through college doing all sorts of jobs.

I started as a receptionist at a large company in Leeds and spent the day answering the phone. I got to know the managers as I passed through calls and took their messages, and I noticed Mike the Marketing Manager was always incredibly stressed and overworked. Since my job entailed a lot of waiting about, I asked Mike if there was anything I could do to help. Well, the floodgates opened. Before long I was responsible for the sales lists and collating addresses of customers. I often stayed late and learned a lot about marketing communications. Then, Mike took me on as a full time marketing assistant and gave me a large charity project to manage.

Some colleagues were suspicious and jealous and I had to win them over, others were really encouraging and took me under their wing. I remember Gladys being one of the encouragers, making sure I got home each evening I worked late, saving me two bus rides and a long walk through the city. I'll always be thankful to her. I left the company on a high with a successful project under my belt, some good experience and numerous job offers enticing me to stay. But my fiancée had a job offer in Surrey and we wanted to be together.

Once we'd moved south, I enrolled onto a part-time Marketing Postgraduate course and began looking for a job. We lived in one mouldy room above a dubious bakery in a small town called Alton while we looked for somewhere more suitable to rent. Again I signed up with an agency which found me a job at a huge company, and I hoped that I might work my way into a permanent job there. Unfortunately, only two days into my admin role, I magically deleted a whole seventy-six page document. To this day, I'm sure I wasn't the culprit (they should have made a back-up anyway) but I took it on the chin and began looking for another job. Thankfully, the agency didn't give up on me and eventually I landed a permanent marketing assistant role. Phew! A bit of tenacity, a lot of resilience and just a pinch of righteous anger got me through that extremely challenging year!

The truth is, that while I was masquerading as a swan in a (somewhat) sophisticated suit and smart heels, I was paddling madly inside. I knew I had to step out and that it would be hard, but the alternative was even more frightening; to be trapped in a world of fear and the feeling of failure. So, I survived by wearing an exterior armour, pretending to be tougher than I really was. I struggled with not seeing my family; I depended so much on my partner that I couldn't socialise without him. Despite people seeing my potential, I didn't see it and I spent many agonising nights worrying and fighting depression.

It was during these times that I called out to God for help. I tried going to a few churches, but nobody spoke to me and I felt awkward. I really felt that God had forgotten me. Looking back I can now see this wasn't true. They may not have been Christians, but God put some great people alongside me. I had an amazing boss and she really took care of me, teaching me everything she knew. I admired her sincerity and her sense of justice. She protected me fiercely and taught me so much about accountability and leadership. I met people through my work who have become life-long friends and very dear to me. Some of my closest friends would not call themselves Christians, and I think it's so important to remember that God loves them just as much as He loves his followers and will use them for His work.

———

DON'T GIVE UP

If we want to achieve something badly enough (and God has given us that deep-rooted passion) we can achieve it, but we will need to be prepared to put in enormous amounts of effort and to experience set-backs. During Nikki's work as a consultant she encountered many people who wanted to change their career direction and spoke passionately about moving into new territory, but only a handful were prepared to put in the work which often entailed hours of preparation, research and even unpaid work experience. Whatever we are prepared to put in we will get back in bucket loads. God really does honour and reward hard work and it does a lot for our self-respect and confidence.

BITESIZE BIBLE BITS

"Careful planning puts you ahead in the long run; hurry and scurry puts you further behind."

- Proverbs 21: 5

"We plan the way we want to live, but only God makes us able to live it."

- Proverbs 16:9 (MSG)

CASE STUDY – LISA'S STORY

Growing up I fell in love with performing arts and I trained to become a singer and dancer in the industry. It took a lot of hard work and determination to persevere through hard times and be dedicated and disciplined in the arts. I trained most weekday evenings and on the weekends. It took hours of practising to be a performer. My identity and confidence were in the skills of singing and dancing. I didn't know who I was underneath the mask I wore. I poured my time, energy and effort into performing arts and worked within entertainment for 10 years in the UK and Europe. However, within this time, I wasn't fully satisfied in life. I was very lost and very afraid.

When I began to follow Jesus, my whole life changed. I still worked as a performer, but it wasn't my core identity anymore. Suddenly, I was experiencing real love from God, and He wasn't pressuring me to perform perfectly every day. My worth wasn't in whether I hit a high note or danced the choreography to perfection. My worth is now in Jesus, He has saved my life and He continues to reveal His love to me daily. In following Jesus, I learnt to dance in freedom again and sing a song of praise from my soul. I still sing and dance and I am grateful for the skills I have learnt, but my identity and confidence is now found in my God.

––––––

MAKE A PLAN

Making a plan is very biblical and there are many verses that refer to planning. Even having a rough idea of what you want to achieve is a great start, and plans can always be updated as time passes and circumstances change. Your plan doesn't have to be written; it might be a personal video or a voice recording, but it does need to be easily accessed so you can come back to it in the future to check you're on target or to make changes if you're not.

1. Record a list of the things you are good at - these can be anything from attributes like being organised or sociable, or skills like drawing or being good at maths.
2. Now record a list of the things you enjoy doing, however basic. For example: eating good food, mountain climbing, writing poetry, travelling.
3. Now write down your dream. Don't limit yourself and don't even think about whether or not it's achievable right now. Just dream big.
4. Now, with that dream in mind, imagine yourself in five years' time. Record what you will be doing. Do the same again, but imagine yourself in ten years' time.
5. Record the steps you need to take to achieve your dream.
6. Give the whole thing to God. He knows the desires of your heart and can help you to achieve this.
7. Take the first step.

It is a good idea to share your dreams with a trusted adult as they can often help you to put your plans into motion, but don't be put off if at first you're met with discouragement. Sometimes we have to convince our parents/carers/loved ones of our commitment and the legitimacy of our intentions - especially if they have other plans for us that don't fit with our own. The people who love us are usually only worried for our wellbeing and we should listen to both their encouraging advice and their reservations.

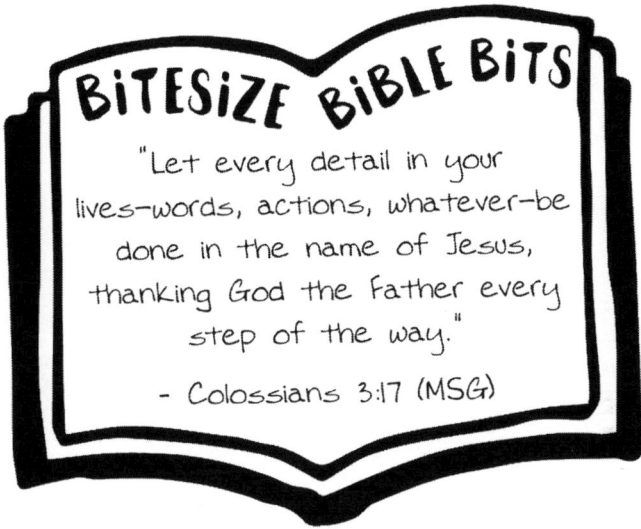

BiTESiZE BiBLE BiTS

"Let every detail in your lives—words, actions, whatever—be done in the name of Jesus, thanking God the Father every step of the way."

- Colossians 3:17 (MSG)

———

Dear Lord

You tell me in your word that you have plans for me, plans to take care of me and to give me the future I hope for (Jeremiah 29:11). I give all my plans over to you now and pray that you will lead me and help me to achieve all that you have for me. I thank you for the opportunities you have given me, for the talents you have bestowed on me and the love with which you surround me. Give me the wisdom to use my abilities well so that I will accomplish my purpose. Protect me from doubt and fear of failure, and from falling into the trap of comparison, and help me to keep my eyes on You.

Amen.

CHAPTER 6
My Disabilities

WE DECIDED to dedicate a whole chapter to My Disabilities because having a disability can have a deep negative impact on our confidence; yet actually our disabilities can often make us stronger in ways we could never imagine.

There are many inspiring books that have been written by people with quite significant disabilities. They have found a way to maximise their potential and have been able to excel despite the hardships and many challenges they face. Nick Vujicic is one of our favourite personalities. He is a motivational speaker and has worked with adults and children alike, spreading the word that God has a plan for everyone and whatever your circumstance, you can achieve it. You see, Nick was born without limbs. Despite this he plays cricket, he's a champion surfer, he has a gorgeous wife and four kids.

In fact, Nick would be one of those people you would say "had it all". However, there were times in his life, especially during his teenage years, when he wanted to end it all. He couldn't see a future for someone like him. He went through horrible bullying at school, he thought he'd never be able to have a normal, intimate relationship, he suffered with terrible depression and at times it seemed that life was impossible. You see, it wasn't all hunky dory for Nick. He did have a family that supported him, but many people outside of his family home were unkind and dismissive. He has written many inspiring books including his life story: *Life without Limits: Inspiration for a Ridiculously Good Life*. He is honest and incredibly inspiring.

NUGGET OF TRUTH

I'm healthily aware of my disabilities but choose to focus on my abilities.

Have you ever watched the Paralympics, listened to the Kaos Signing Choir, or read about business gurus who have battled with ME, dyslexia or mental illness? You try telling these disabled people they can't do it. They have all succeeded and will continue to reach their full potential if that is what they want to do. We can do the same.

Perhaps those of us with a disability have listened to the negative voices telling us we are worth less than the average person. It is only our world's culture that tells us that if you're born anything other than 'normal', you have a disability! Who decided what was normal?

. . .

God can make good out of any situation. He does not see things the way we see them. He sees each of us as a precious, specially formed individual. Everyone has a purpose, passions, likes and dislikes; we all have the ability to love, to be kind.

BIBLICAL DISABILITIES

Let's have a look at some people in the Bible who might have been considered disabled in some way.

Moses complained that he didn't have good speech. He asked God to send someone in his place because of his speech impediment. Of course God said no, because he knew that He would make sure Moses had everything he needed for this mission. However, he did allow Moses to take his brother Aaron to support him. (Exodus 4:10-16)

Then there was Mephibosheth, Jonathan's son, who was dropped as a baby and became disabled. He described himself as a "dead dog" yet he got married, had a son, became King Saul's sole heir and was granted a permanent seat at King David's table. He was not a nobody, he was a somebody. (2 Samuel 9)

Paul in the New Testament complained about being in torment. He describes his torment as a "thorn in his flesh" and has begged God to take it from him a number of times. We can only guess what ailed him but it was something that really affected him, enough to give him pain and torment. Paul came to the conclusion that his disability made him draw closer to God. It kept him humble and reminded him that God was his strength and not to lean on his own strength too much. (2 Corinthians 12:7-10)

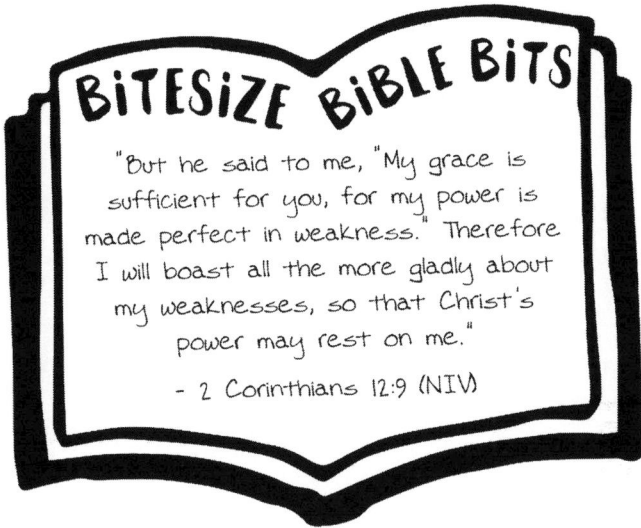

BITESIZE BIBLE BITS

"But he said to me, "My grace is sufficient for you, for my power is made perfect in weakness." Therefore I will boast all the more gladly about my weaknesses, so that Christ's power may rest on me."

- 2 Corinthians 12:9 (NIV)

HEALING

God doesn't cause pain or suffering, yet as Christians, we are told to expect it. There are many theologies on healing, pain and suffering, and so much reading material around the subject, but for me it is very simple. God made us and he loves us. When we get to heaven we will be given new bodies and there won't be pain or suffering. We can assume that God never intended us to suffer this way, it's just the state of the world we live in. God is a healer, a creator, He is love, He is good. He can make a very difficult situation a good one, though it might not look the way we imagine. We don't have all the answers and, for many of us, perhaps we won't get them until we face the Creator. However, we won't stop praying and asking for healing.

NIKKI'S STORY

Ari was diagnosed with a brain condition at the age of nine months. Suddenly the future for my beautiful baby daughter appeared to be very bleak. We were told that she wouldn't walk or talk and to expect the very worst outcome for her. As you can imagine we were devastated and confused. You see, Ari was such a prayed-for baby. Months before her conception we had been praying for her, all the way through my pregnancy she was healthy and doing well, and literally two weeks before her diagnosis, she was baptised into the church family. Why would God do this? I would be lying if I told you I just accepted this all as God's will. In fact, to this day I do not believe it is God's will to suffer with sickness and ill health. For a short time, I was filled with anger and disappointment and I turned my back on God.

Then, I realised I had a choice. Live totally without God or live fully with Him. It changed my whole view of who I am in Christ. Suddenly the Bible was either true or not true at all, as this holy book is the only tangible thing we have that belongs to God. (It can't be both – what's the point of it being God's word if some of it isn't true? And, anyway, who would decide which bits are true and which bits aren't?) I also decided that if God's word was true, then I needed to find out who God is (and was and will be). So, to cut a lengthy story very short I embarked on an extensive journey discovering God and where my daughter's diagnosis fit in with it all.

Ari has just reached sixteen, and all of us (Ari, my husband, my son and me) have all been through a journey (in fact we're still on it!). The world wants to slap all sorts of labels on Ari but actually she is who she is: Ari. To the outside world Ari is a young person who has additional needs and is unable to contribute to society. To God and to all of us who know her, she is so much more and probably contributes more than the average person.

Ari is kind, gentle and has a great love for Jesus. She can speak and can walk. She has this amazing ability to love and empathise with people. Her hugs alone reduce people to tears (in a good way) and she has impacted many people in their lives, lifting them from sadness, giving them a new direction, helping them to re-evaluate and reshape their lives. I can see that God uses her in so many ways to build His Kingdom here on earth.

NUGGET OF TRUTH

Everyone has a God given purpose. Everyone.

IS IT HIDDEN?

Globally, one in seven of us lives with a disability. And of those disabilities, 80% are invisible. That is one billion people who are living with a non-visible disability. That is a lot of people! These hidden disabilities are not immediately obvious to the people around us. They can be physical, mental or neurological and include autism, cognitive learning difficulties, dementia, speech impediments, visual impairments, hearing loss, depression, chronic insomnia. The list is endless and though they are not easily seen, they all can have a serious impact on our lives.

Having children who masked their struggles and desperately tried to fit themselves into a busy, unforgiving world, has been an eye-opener for us. We both wish we'd been more aware of the challenges they were facing so we could have been more supportive at the beginning of their struggles; but now, with the research that is available, we have all been able to gain greater understanding and to discover how they tick. It has been humbling to have our children teach and equip us. It has been amazing how this has led to so many conversations with other people about their hidden disabilities.

We want you to know that your disability may be 'hidden' but God sees the whole, real you. The people who love you can do this too, and so can you! Look in the mirror, really look and see yourself. And remember, in your deepest, darkest moments when you feel far away from God and hidden from the world, He sees you. He hears you. And He is delighted in you.

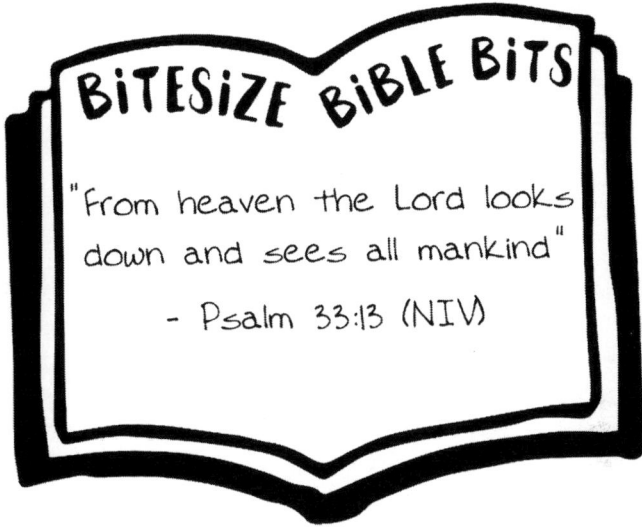

BITESIZE BIBLE BITS

"From heaven the Lord looks down and sees all mankind"

- Psalm 33:13 (NIV)

SARAH'S STORY

This summer of 2021, I sat glued to the Paralympics. The Olympics were great and I enjoyed the achievements of Great Britain, but for some reason, this year, the Paralympics resonated more with me. Perhaps it was that Covid had put so many restrictions on life? There was so much that we couldn't do as a society, so many things that we were not allowed to do, or felt a trepidation about doing, and perhaps for some of us that sense of a shrinking world put up barriers around us saying 'I can't, I don't want to, I shouldn't.'

However, for me watching the Paralympics, the swimming in particular (and I hate swimming!), I was inspired. I was awestruck by the determination, the talent and the training of the competitors. One thing that struck me was the beauty of the swimming styles that had been adopted by some of the athletes according to their specific physical disabilities. The way they had adapted strokes, techniques and movement through the water was breathtaking. These athletes had not allowed their disability to limit them, but had actually used it to push them forward. A potentially small, forbidden world had been obliterated due to their attitude, determination and skill. Often we focus on the things we can't do and allow that to define us – but thank goodness God doesn't. He sees the real you. The you who has so much to offer the world and who is unique. The you who can bring joy and blessing to others.

My mum had a wonderful friend, Elizabeth, who was blind. As a child, I remember her coming regularly with her faithful guide dog to our house for tea and cake. I enjoyed listening to them chatting and laughing together, and would often sneak into the lounge (which had the most hideous 70's orange and brown carpet) to steal a piece of my mum's flapjack and stroke the dog's silky ears. One day, Elizabeth gave me a book in braille and showed me how to read it.

I used to wonder what it must be like to be without sight. I thought of all the things that she couldn't see, or do – but she seemed to have the opposite focus. She would regale us with tales about her adventures, the wonderful opportunities she'd been given and how her other heightened senses had made her experiences even more powerful. She was a lady full of joy and excitement, exuding love and support to all those around her. She knew her identity in God and had a true sense of purpose and worth. No matter how the world judged her as disabled, she did not define herself by her disability. Yes, she was blind but she was also so much more. Her wisdom had such an impact on me.

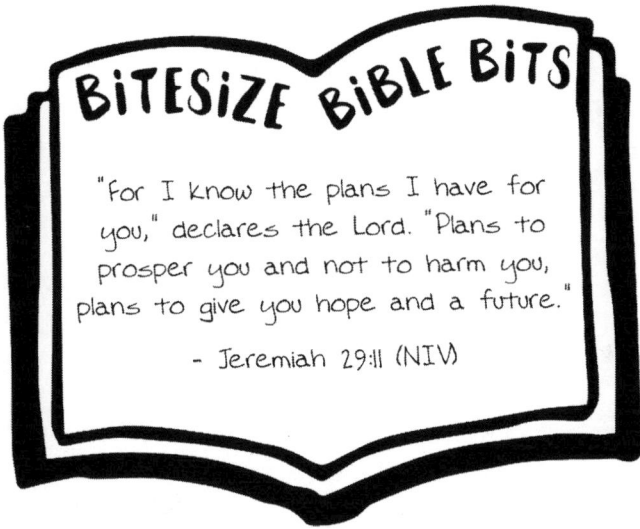

BITESIZE BIBLE BITS

"For I know the plans I have for you," declares the Lord. "Plans to prosper you and not to harm you, plans to give you hope and a future."

- Jeremiah 29:11 (NIV)

DANIELLE'S STORY

When I was a baby, mum and dad adopted both me and my brother. They told my mum I would never sit up, walk or talk but I can do all of these things! I love my mum and dad and they will always be my real parents and I lived with them and three brothers and two sisters until I moved into my flat two years ago. During all of my childhood, I went to special school but I preferred the sixth form because we went out to town to do shopping and to Spud Club where we would buy, prepare and cook potatoes to sell to people. I loved my teachers because they were friendly and they helped me.

. . .

Now, I live by myself in an assisted flat which means that I can call helpers who help me when I need it. They take me to the shops, help me with cooking, order my medication and everyday things like that. Twice a week, I go to the day centre where I meet my friends. We do activities like yoga and dancing and we go on outings like bowling. At first, I was very nervous and wouldn't go out anywhere with them but they really helped me to become more confident in myself and my own ability.

In the evenings I go to a drama club. We have written a play about dreams and we are practising for the show to start in October. I have a singing part. I never used to be very confident and would have never got up on a stage but one day, I was at a BBQ and some friends persuaded me to sing with them. Everyone said I had a lovely voice and told me I should sing. I never thought I'd ever be able to sing in front of people. Then, a few weeks later, my church worship leader heard about my voice and asked if I would sing in the worship team. I was really scared and didn't want to be up in front of everyone but slowly, over time and with lots of encouragement from my friends, I became braver. I can't read but if someone reads the words out to me, I can easily memorise them. Now, I love singing in the worship team and don't mind people looking at me.

Every Sunday I go to church and spend time with God and my friends. I can't remember not having God in my life but mum tells me that when I was in my late teens I came downstairs and told her that Jesus had been with me in my bedroom. She said that it was from then my faith became strong.

• • •

I know some people might judge me and think that I can't do much because I need a lot of help and can't always do things by myself but God knows me. He's given me a voice to worship him and a good memory so I can remember the words. I'm a little bit wary of people until I get to know them but once I do, I like to make them happy.

———

BE WHO YOU ARE!

Be your own advocate – you are best placed to know what you need, enjoy and find challenging. Educate yourself and your nearest and dearest about your rights and the resources that are available to you. Taking charge of who you are can be hugely empowering.

Set realistic goals, and be patient – a disability may force you to learn new skills and strategies, it may mean you have to be creative in the way you get things done. You might have to do things differently or at a different pace to your peers. This can be frustrating, but be patient with yourself.

Nurture the important relationships in your life – staying connected with others is essential to your wellbeing. Find 'your' people and hold them close. Be honest with them and let them see 'the real you'. Spending time with good family and friends is so important, and they will help to lift you on those difficult days. Ensure that the people around you are the people who build you up, not drag you down.

. . .

Join a club or group – finding a place where you feel you can be truly *you* can be a huge help. Knowing that you are not alone goes a long way.

Develop hobbies that make you happy. Find things that you love and that bring you joy and get stuck in, whether it is craft, sport, singing, dancing, gaming, reading, watching football, looking after a pet. Whatever it is, do it and have fun doing it.

BITESIZE BIBLE BITS

"So we're not giving up. How could we! Even though on the outside it often looks like things are falling apart on us, on the inside, where God is making new life, not a day goes by without His unfolding grace."

- 2 Corinthians 4:16 (MSG)

Heavenly Father

You knit each one of us together with care and love. We commit ourselves to you; our bodies, our minds, our hopes and our dreams. We trust that you will show us our gifts and talents and help us to use them for Your good. Protect us from all negative language and actions that are not from You. Help us to remember that nothing is impossible for you and that we can achieve anything that you have put into our deepest desires.

Amen

CHAPTER 7
My Image

LET'S BE HONEST, our image and what people think of us is important to most of us. It takes an exceptionally courageous person to hand-on-heart declare they do not care what anyone thinks about them. We care about hair, clothes, jewellery, fashion brands, the types of people we are seen with, the clubs we frequent, even the type of mobile phone we have! Apparently it takes a mere seven seconds for someone to form an impression of us, and we want people to accept and like us.

When Nikki was a teen, her mum loved to shop in second hand shops and she dreaded being seen by the kids from school who would mock her second hand clothes. Nowadays it's trendy to shop at second hand stores; but the point is she didn't want to appear different or weird. She longed to be like everyone else. Some of us will even hide our hobbies and special interests for fear of ridicule. Imagine if anyone discovered we love playing chess, building model aeroplanes and tap dancing! Seriously, there is nothing wrong with these activities and everything wrong with being embarrassed to do the things we love.

The school years are tough and we all long to fit in without ridicule or even comment, so we keep our heads down and try to survive; but the trick is to survive without losing sight of who we are created to be. And honestly, God doesn't want us to merely survive: He wants us to live wholeheartedly and to reach our full potential.

God made each and every one of us. He carved out our uniqueness with love and pride. We have our own opinions, beliefs, boundaries, principles and views and we are entitled to them. We should stand up for who we are and what we believe in, and not be brow-beaten into thinking and being what we believe everyone else wants us to be. Yes, we may want people to think well of us, but not before we have accepted and liked ourselves first.

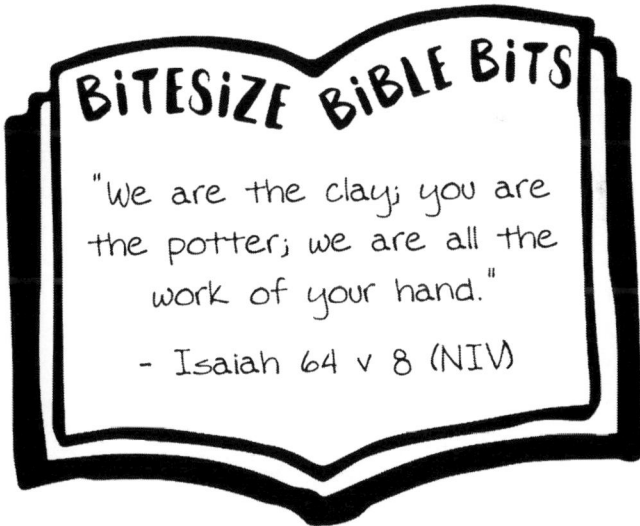

BITESIZE BIBLE BITS

"We are the clay; you are the potter; we are all the work of your hand."

- Isaiah 64 v 8 (NIV)

NIKKI'S STORY

During my teen years, mum warned me against becoming someone who simply followed the herd to fit in. I hated being tall and I wanted to be the same height as everyone else (you try making yourself shorter!) I longed to wear the same clothes (even if they didn't suit me), to be allowed to have the same privileges (my friends always seemed to have more freedom) and I hated appearing different. Slowly, I came to realise that being the same as everyone else is not a good thing. Hiding my light behind all the other bodies also trying to hide did me no good whatsoever; but at the same time I get that it is hard to stick your head above the parapet (unless you're six foot like me!)

Eventually I gave up wishing I was shorter. God made me this way and I could either act ashamed and embarrassed or I could just get on with it. I decided to wear heels (I really loved the clickety-clack sound of heels) and I pretended not to care that I was taller than the boy I fancied. Before I knew it, I really didn't care and basically if any potential boyfriend had a problem with it, then it was *his* problem.

Our image isn't just about the way we look, it is also very much about the way we act. Sometimes we act in ways that are not healthy for us (or anybody else) because we want to fit in. Again, it's that herd mentality my mum used to nag me about. Be proud to be you! God made me to be me, and being like someone else is not His best for me. Pretending to agree with someone, or acting like them just so they will like us, is not only fooling them but it is also fooling ourselves. Our uniqueness is our strength and it makes us awesome!

NUGGET OF TRUTH

Be yourself.
True friends will love you for yourself.

PEER PRESSURE

Pressure and influence from peers can come in a number of forms and affects every one of us. However, the age when someone is at their most impressionable (and vulnerable) is during the middle school years when children are making new friends and choosing their identity around these friends. This might also be the time when some kids experiment with alcohol, drugs, sexual activity and other risky behaviours.

There are six main forms of peer pressure: spoken and unspoken, direct and indirect and positive and negative.

Direct peer pressure can be spoken or unspoken and might include something like someone handing a person an alcoholic drink or verbally persuading someone to wear something offensive. It can be done in a group or on a one to one basis.

Indirect peer pressure is much more subtle, but just as effective, as it can involve a person without them realising they are taking part. For example, you might overhear someone gossiping about a friend, and you find yourself agreeing or even adding more gossip.

• • •

However, there is also positive peer pressure, and this is most effective in a group: for example if a youth club agree they won't have alcohol at any of their parties, other people may hear about this and feel confident enough to do the same.

Our peers are so important to us, but they are not the only examples we have. When we are young, our carers, parents and older siblings can be a powerful influence in our lives. Judgement-free open dialogue, modelling responsible behaviour and supporting healthy relationships can help us all to make great decisions and protect us from any negative peer pressure.

———

A NOTE ON PORNOGRAPHY, SEX AND OTHER STUFF

A recent research study* showed that over 66% of teens aged between 14 and 15 have seen porn, and that watching pornography from the age of 16 onwards is becoming normalised due to smart phone use. There is a lot of evidence to suggest that pornography is harmful, especially to young people who are trying to make sense of sex, love and relationships, because it gives a very twisted, degraded view of sex. Sex was created to be meaningful and beautiful, to be enjoyed by two people who love each other; yet this multi-billion dollar industry is invading our lives through social media, persuading us that pornography is just a harmless little bit of fun. Push ads and notifications appear telling us we need to be sexually exciting and interesting, and we need to buy this or do that to attract potential partners. This industry is clever and plays on naivety, lack of confidence and youthful innocence.

. . .

Being strong and saying, "no" can take a lot of courage due to potential criticism and scorn, but in the end people will begin to respect you for your choice. Generation Z is all about freedom of choice, expression and the recognition of a gender spectrum. People have the freedom to state their orientation or preference, so perhaps it is more acceptable now than ever before to say no to having sex or engaging in sexual activity, especially if you are unsure or feel you are being pressured. Whilst in some ways choice can be hazardous and confusing, in other ways it can be quite liberating. The important thing is for us not to be co-coerced or bullied into making a choice or decision. Learning to say "no" and "not now" can be beneficial, even if only to give ourselves more time to establish what choices are right for us and what might do us harm.

*carried out by British Board of Film Classification

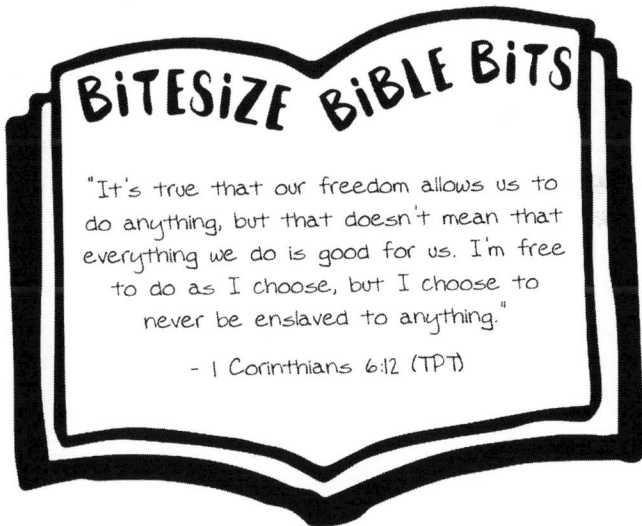

BITESIZE BIBLE BITS

"It's true that our freedom allows us to do anything, but that doesn't mean that everything we do is good for us. I'm free to do as I choose, but I choose to never be enslaved to anything."

- 1 Corinthians 6:12 (TPT)

SARAH'S STORY

We go to such lengths to avoid judgement from others and to fit in, don't we? As a teenager, I never really felt that I fitted in. I was kind of awkward – I didn't really know who I was. I worked hard at school and always did as I was told (one of my nicknames was 'Squara') but I wasn't wholly part of that group in school. I played on some sports teams so occasionally the 'cool' girls spoke to me – but I certainly wasn't one of them. I was quite confident in some respects, but I was definitely masking a lot of insecurities - and my appearance? Well, I tried to wear what was 'in trend' but never quite managed to pull it off. In essence, I guess I never really could grasp who I was and where I fitted.

I suppose I was pretty much trying to be like a chameleon. I wanted to fit in, and I wanted to be liked (not necessarily popular, just liked). So, like a chameleon changes its colour to hide their emotions or to fit in with its surroundings, I too would do the same. I would adapt to match the surroundings I found myself in at the time, and to fit in with the different groups of people I was with. I would have a mask (or an image) for each group, slickly changing it when and where necessary. To some extent this was successful and actually a useful skill. However, I still struggle in my adult years with being me and worry about fitting in. As we grow older, it is important to be able to act in particular ways for interviews and in jobs, which may be different to how you are with your friends on a night out, but it shouldn't be about changing the person you are.

At secondary school, I had a friend called Mel. She was a talented actress and had a beautiful singing voice. She spoke her mind and never doubted her opinions, and when it came to her image – she was unique. She dressed very differently to everyone else in the school and certainly stood out in a crowd.

I admired her confidence; comfortable in her own style. Although the way she dressed, her appearance and make-up were not what I personally liked, I wish in hindsight I could have been more like her. She knew who she was, was confident with her image and ignored the people who didn't like it. Mel didn't want or feel the need to 'fit in' with the different groups at school like I did. She knew that people would either like her for all her qualities or they wouldn't, and this didn't bother her. Wherever she is now, I do hope she is still the same straight-talking, gifted, and self-assured person that she was when she was 17.

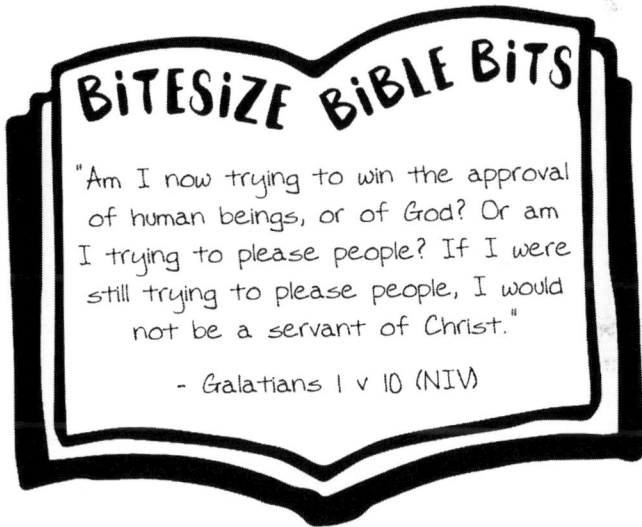

BITESIZE BIBLE BITS

"Am I now trying to win the approval of human beings, or of God? Or am I trying to please people? If I were still trying to please people, I would not be a servant of Christ."

- Galatians 1 v 10 (NIV)

CASE STUDY – JACOB'S STORY

It's hard to be brave. I should know. I have anxiety and started secondary school in 2020. I was really nervous about it and just wanted to fit in. I had no idea who anyone was and now was expected to do a lot more. It was a lot stricter and I was dreading every day and literally trying to do anything to get out of it. I would even take my temperature every day in case I was ill and wouldn't have to go to school. And I would get stressed because of stupid things as well. Like I wanted to get out of my chair without making any noise or I would walk down the wrong corridor and then walk all around the school just so people wouldn't see me change direction. It took ages but I was finally getting into the swing of things when Covid hit. And everything just reset. But now I'm ok. It's been a while so I've made friends who are now all asking me for advice on how to talk to people. The trick is, just pretend like you know what you're doing and you will be fine. It does not matter if you have no idea and feel just as clueless as me. If you don't pretend to be someone else and just be who you are around people, real friends will like you for it.

––––––

WHAT DO YOU IMMERSE YOURSELF IN?

Did you know that whatever we spend most of our time doing, reading, listening to or watching will have the most effect on us? It will influence our morals, our values, our beliefs; it will impact our decisions, our plans for the future, in fact it will influence our whole life. Just as hours of painting and drawing will hone your artistry skills, watching fourteen seasons of your favourite Netflix drama will craft your outlook on life. Before long, you will find yourself mirroring the characters' mannerisms, language and perhaps even habits! Simply put, we will become whatever we immerse ourselves in.

THE SOCIAL MEDIA BATTLE

On social media, we spend our lives looking at small snapshots of other people's lives and making assumptions about who they are, what they are like and how they live, based on the images which they share. Studies show that people who lack confidence in themselves and their image spend the most time on social media, and this can cause them to have even lower self-esteem. This means that people who are already lacking confidence are indulging in something that can make it worse. It is a vicious cycle and one which is really tricky to get out of.

Our image tells a story, but what story does your image tell? In a world of stereotypes, it is important to recognise that image isn't simply about how we appear on the outside, it is also about how we feel on the inside. We need to surround ourselves with people who value us for who we are and not just for who we appear to be.

NUGGET OF TRUTH

When I see an advert, I ask myself, "What lies are they telling me?"

WHY DO I FEEL SO JUDGED?

Let's face it, humans judge. It is an instinctive behaviour that is within us all. Judgement affects our perspective of our image and our confidence. The conclusions people make about us may be 'good' or 'bad' but they are there, and no one is free from receiving or making them. As we get to know someone, our minds reassess those initial judgements. It is an ongoing process. However, because of this we tend to go to all sorts of lengths to avoid the possibility of being negatively judged by others. We change how we look to fit in, we alter the language we use so we are part of the 'group,' we dress differently, act differently, behave differently, and engage in different habits. We may hide our past or lie about what we have done – all to avoid this idea of being judged, but ultimately judgement will always come.

> *See that boy, over there,*
> *Don't like his clothes, don't like his hair,*
> *I make him cry, but I don't care,*
> *He's different to me.*
> *See that boy, over there,*
> *He isn't kind, he isn't fair*
> *He makes me sad, but I'm aware*
> *I'm not different, I'm just me.*

(Imogen Buxton-Pickles from iMoves.com – rap written for anti-bullying week 2021)

―――――

SOON FORGOTTEN

We cannot control the judgements others make in their first impression of us – they're being influenced by their own experiences and prejudices. But the good news is that the memories of their initial judgement of us will not be significant enough to be stored in their long-term memory. To be honest, people don't care about our identity and appearance as much as we do, because they are too busy worrying about their own image.

Those fleeting judgements we make are just that, fleeting. We do not need to chase approval from others; we need to chase approval from ourselves.

———

YOU AND ONLY YOU

The only person who knows the absolute truth about you is you (and God). Of course, people will have opinions but you must try to hold on to the truth and have faith in who you are and what God has created you to be. Don't let another's image of you become your reality.

READING MINDS

If we do not have complete trust and confidence in who we are and our actions, we can sometimes imagine disapproval from others which is not even there! This can make us alter who we are and it's all for nothing! Let's not try to read someone else's mind. In fact, in doing so, we are the ones making the judgement! Seek approval from just one place.

———

FORGIVENESS IS KEY

Harbouring resentment over people's thoughts and perceptions of us has absolutely no effect on anyone other than ourselves. We must learn to forgive those opinions, forgive the wrong judgements and free ourselves from being bound by the hurt.

LET PEOPLE SEE YOU

Judgements can be hurtful but they are brief. Our identity and our image is so much more than those fleeting thoughts from others. Let people see you, the real you. Let them appreciate who you are and what makes you unique. Allow people to get to know you. Our image is more than just what we look like: our image is about our beliefs, our actions, our thoughts, and our attitudes. Take off your mask and let people see you just like God sees you.

———

Dear Lord

Sometimes I doubt myself and listen to others' opinions about me. Help me to remember that you created me to be me and that You love me as I am. Protect me from the things that can harm me and affect my image in a negative way, and help me to recognise the voices that are there to derail me. Surround me with people who love me and want Your best for me. Set me on your path to accomplish everything you have for me and to be all that you created me to be.

Amen

CHAPTER 8
My Friendships

FRIENDSHIPS FORM an important part of our identity and have a huge impact on how we build future relationships. Particularly during our teenage years, our relationships can matter more to us than family. As young children we were less picky and simply moved from group to group to play alongside the person who had the most interesting toy or who we thought was having the most fun. But as we get older our connections become deeper and much more significant in our navigation of life. There is also evidence to suggest that teenagers who do have close friendships experience a greater sense of self-worth and, interestingly, it is not the number of relationships that is important but the strength of one relationship. (Rachel K. Narr, 2019)

Humans are inherently social creatures – our whole scientific make-up is wired to belong, and in our increasingly digital world, we need connection more than ever. Sadly, it is becoming more common to receive 'likes' on social media than face-to-face compliments, and due to the recent pandemic, life has become even more isolated. More than ever, we need real connection. Nicole K McNichols PhD (Psychologytoday.-

com/gb/blog/everyone-top/202108/the-vital-importance-human-touch) states "It is scientifically proven that the need for human touch is one of our most basic, primal needs. Touch deprivation is correlated with negative health outcomes such as anxiety, depression, and immune system disorders."

NUGGET OF TRUTH

I've heard that new born babies can experience healing when in skin-to-skin contact with their mothers - when I am hugged by a good friend, I can believe it.

HAVING FRIENDS IS HEALTHY

Often, our teenage years revolve around the need for romantic relationships. We might think that finding 'the one' or even 'anyone' who loves us is the greatest thing ever. We might think finding a partner will make us happy, fulfilled and confident. We may mistakenly believe being in a romantic relationship makes us more popular, attractive and worthy than others, and if we are not in a relationship (and most of our peers are), we might begin to worry we are not good enough. Finding a partner may bring us a degree of confidence, but research shows that true friends are far more important to our psychological welfare. Friends bring more happiness into our lives than virtually anything else.

. . .

Friendships have a huge impact on our mental health and happiness. Good friends relieve stress, provide comfort and joy, prevent loneliness and isolation and boost our confidence in becoming the individual that we are designed to be. A friend will support you through tough times, laugh with you and cry with you and when all else fails – eat chocolate with you!

But close friendships rarely just happen. They have to be built over time as we earn each other's trust, share vulnerabilities and understand each other's character until we build that *philia* love (that's Greek for the love of friends and equals). Nevertheless, for some of us this can be difficult (especially if we have been betrayed, traumatised, or abused in the past and we may need specialist support). Social anxiety is a real thing and many of us struggle to meet people at all, let alone develop good, quality connections. We're afraid we don't fit - that we're too different, even weird - but the worst thing we can do is isolate ourselves. If this happens and we begin to slip into a negative state of mind - or, worse, depression - we MUST seek help.

As any teen knows, spending some time alone can be good for us, give us space to think things through and time to recharge; but too much time can be damaging. God did not intend human beings to be truly solitary, and the teen years will be lonely without a support network of people who 'get us'.

BITESIZE BIBLE BITS

"Some friendships do not last, but some friends are more loyal than brothers."

- Proverbs 18:24 (GNT)

NIKKI'S STORY - PART ONE

As a child I was shy and quiet and had little confidence in myself. I changed school quite a few times, and though I usually had someone to 'hang around with' I didn't really have 'best friends' until around the age of eleven. Jane and I became firm friends for about two years until our relationship fizzled out when my family moved abroad. We shared everything from our most precious possessions to our hopes and dreams and we would have probably shared our clothes if it wasn't for the fact I was the tallest girl in the class and she was the shortest. We completely trusted each other and were able to totally be ourselves in each other's company, which might be why I wasn't always the best sort of friend because I took her for granted.

. . .

In fact, one thing in particular haunts me to this day; a time when I really could have been a better friend. My dad had dropped us off at the leisure centre for a couple of hours' swimming. We had a great time in the pool, dunking each other, repeatedly jumping into the deep end and generally having fun, oblivious to anyone else around us, until it was time to shower and get changed.

The showers were large communal ones and at first we had the block to ourselves with Jane's bottles of shampoo, conditioner and shower gel lined up on the floor for us to share. All of a sudden, four older girls piled in and one of them started to make fun of us with all our bottles. Recognising a bully when I saw one (I was badly bullied in primary school) I shrank back hoping I wouldn't be noticed, and began to rinse out shampoo as quickly as I could but Jane just carried on like she didn't have a care in the world. The bully picked up one of the bottles and tipped it up, proceeding to empty it of its contents and then moved onto the next bottle. Jane must have said something because the bully, egged on by the others, laughed and taunted her some more and finally emptied the last bottle. Jane continued to complain and tried to get her bottle back, but I just stood there and said nothing. But that isn't the worst bit. As the bully threw the bottle down she grinned at me and I *smiled* back.

Yep! You heard right, I smiled as though to encourage the bully. The truth is I was terrified of those horrible girls turning their attention on me, but at the expense of letting my best friend take the full impact of their nastiness. They got bored and left us, and Jane just carried on as if nothing had happened. I, on the other hand, felt incredibly ashamed of myself for being a complete coward and the worst sort of friend. We dried off and got dressed, and finally when we were out in the car park waiting for my dad, I couldn't help myself. "Jane," I blurted. "I'm really sorry!"

"Why?" she asked in surprise.

I went on to explain how scared I'd been of those girls. "I should have fought for you. That's what friends do."

But Jane was so forgiving she didn't even think there was anything to forgive. That's a true friend.

———

SO, WHAT IS A GOOD FRIEND?

When we are looking for friends or developing those teenage friendships, it is important to know what a good friend actually looks like. Good friends should have a positive effect on your self-esteem, your interests and your behaviours. They should provide you with a great support network that is in addition to your family. They should be trustworthy and honest and enable you to feel like you can be 100% yourself. Friends should listen without judgement and certainly not pressurise you to be anything other than your authentic self.

This may seem like a tall order, but remember it is never about the quantity of friends; it is, as cheesy as it sounds, about quality. Some of us are lucky enough to find life-long, great friends during our teens. But many of us (as we develop into the person we were designed to be and discover our own beliefs, opinions and values) may find some of our friendships naturally diminish. We grow away from each other and discover we have more in common with others. There may even be times of famine; a friend has moved house, changed schools or simply moved on with their life and we feel disconnected with everyone. But hang on in there! It will not be like this forever.

NUGGET OF TRUTH

A best friend by my side banishes the baddies.

TO HAVE A GOOD FRIEND WE NEED TO BE A GOOD FRIEND

As humans we have an inbuilt mechanism to be quite selfish. This is true too when it comes to friendship. We think about our needs and wants, our self-worth and confidence as well as our ultimate desire to be liked and accepted. This is natural. But we do need to remember that we also have a part to play in our friendships. If we think about what we would like in a friendship, then we should try to be those things for others.

MAKING FRIENDS

Making a new friend is the beginning of the story. But friendships take time to form and develop on a deeper level, so be patient.

- Be the friend that you would like to have. Be reliable, thoughtful, trustworthy and willing to share yourself and your time.
- Be a good listener as well as a sharer. We love the analogy that we have two ears and one mouth, meaning that we should do double the listening than talking.
- Give your friend space. Everyone needs time to be alone or to spend with other friends: your new friend is not solely yours.
- Don't set too many expectations. Allow the friendship to evolve naturally; try not to force things.
- Be forgiving. None of us is perfect. We all make mistakes, and our friends are no exception. There will be disagreements and fall outs and that is ok, but allow them to deepen the friendship, not weaken it.
- Focus on others, not yourself. The key to connecting with others is to show a genuine interest in their thoughts, experiences, and interests. You will make far more friends by showing your interest in them rather than trying to get people interested in you.
- Pay attention. In a digital world when we are with our friends, it's good to switch off phones, avoid distractions and enjoy each other's physical presence.

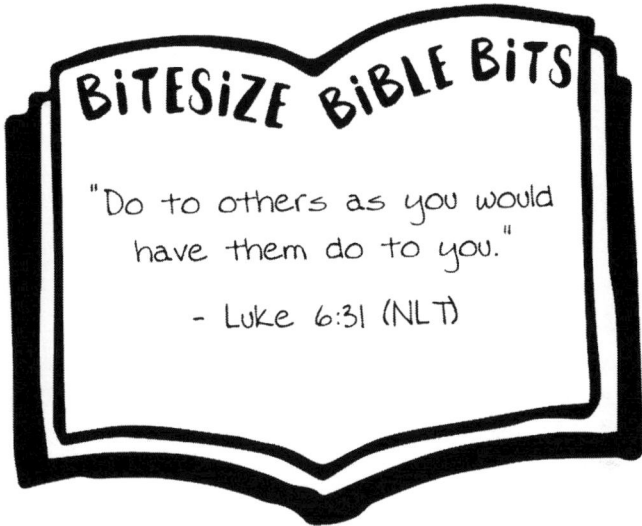

BiTESiZE BiBLE BiTS

"Do to others as you would have them do to you."

- Luke 6:31 (NLT)

SARAH'S STORY

Friendships were difficult for me. If I were to categorise people (I do try not to!) I would have put myself in the 'geek' group. I was well behaved, always handed my homework in on time and was not particularly fashion aware or worldly-wise. My family didn't listen to music much, so growing up I didn't really know 'who was who' in the charts let alone know the lyrics of the songs. I was quite sheltered in terms of what I was allowed to do and watch, and to top it all off - at the age of around 15 - I had the most hideous hairstyle. Looking back at photos now the question 'why?' will leap into my mind! All of these things as a whole were not conducive to being particularly popular. In fact, you might remember one of my nicknames was 'Squara'. (Which I am quite fond of now!)

I continuously felt I didn't quite fit in any one 'group.' I was ok at some sports and scraped my way into the hockey and netball team but I wasn't completely accepted as one of the 'sporty' girls. I had a bit more confidence than some of the shyer 'geeks' and I certainly wasn't ever part of that 'elusive' girl group – the popular ones who always had a boyfriend and everyone admired. On the whole, I always felt more comfortable with boys. I found that these friendships were more straightforward to navigate than those friendships with girls. Although there were a few times of unrequited love when I was 'friend-zoned' by a couple of these boys who I'd begun to fall for slightly.

Throughout my years in school and university I was more of a 'flitter' – I spent short amounts of time with different groups but never really found my true place anywhere. On reflection, I have realised this was probably more about my own personal self-esteem and confidence in who I was, rather than whether those people 'accepted' me or not. Looking back, I was genuinely liked and appreciated by many of the people I spent time with, but my own insecurities held me back from allowing myself to accept their friendship. Now, I realise I should have accepted me for me and allowed people to like me for me. Then those times of loneliness, striving to fit in and internal anguish may have lessened – having said that, this is something I still regularly challenge myself on now.

My husband says he really struggled at school with friendships. His family didn't have a lot of money and things were quite tough. He suffered a lot of bullying both in primary and secondary school. He hated school with a passion and would sometimes hide rather than go to lessons. He was gentle and kind, and had always been taught to 'turn the other cheek', so I guess he was an easy target. I remember him telling me the story of a regular experience as he and his brother cycled home from school. They would set off in a panic, knowing that they had to get to a certain point on the journey home before the school bus passed them. If they managed to reach that point and take shelter, it would avoid the inevitable pelting of stones out of the bus windows onto their heads. School was a lonely place.

However, for both of us we had a saving grace. We were both blessed with friendships outside of our school context. We both (in different parts of the country at the time) were part of churches with thriving youth groups. There we found people who accepted us for who we were, who encouraged us and cared for us and who listened and celebrated our achievements with us. It was not always easy - there were still fallings out and disagreements - but it did provide us both with a sense of belonging which did not exist at school.

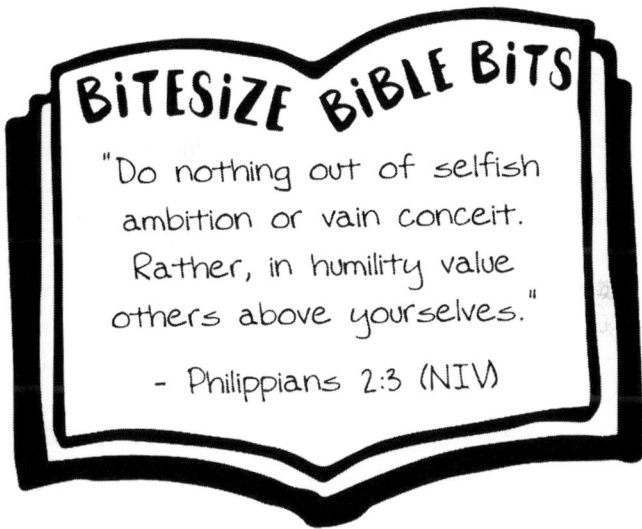

BITESIZE BIBLE BITS

"Do nothing out of selfish ambition or vain conceit. Rather, in humility value others above yourselves."

- Philippians 2:3 (NIV)

CASE STUDY - DAVID'S STORY

By the time I was thirteen years old, I knew I was gay but I struggled. My church was filled with people who were kind and loved God, but being gay was considered a sin. I hated being gay and I begged God to take it away. I'd get down on my knees and plead with him to make me "normal" only to find, a few days later, that I was just the same. I was led to believe that being gay was a sickness or worse, a choice, and I nearly made myself ill worrying that there was something wrong with me or that God didn't love me. To me, the Bible was clear: being gay was wrong.

For twenty six years I chose to ignore that I was gay. I dedicated my life to the church, spending much of my career in community outreach and helping others. To everyone else I was confident, happy, the life and soul. Too busy to commit to a serious relationship. To everyone else I was the perfect Christian, devoted to my work with others. However, on the inside I was a mess, hating myself one minute, and angry at God the next for not 'healing' me. I couldn't go on living in this mental hell forever, and earlier this year, aged thirty nine, I decided enough was enough. I would be honest about who I am.

I told my pastors and they were really supportive, one even exclaiming that if anyone else had a problem with me being gay they would be shown the door. A few friends encouraged me to spread the word of my "coming out" using social media. In rural Lincolnshire, where everyone is white, middle-class and pretty conservative, it was terrifying but I thought that if I could help someone else in a similar situation then I'd do it! To be honest, everyone was nice about it, some even congratulating me in the milk aisle at Sainsburys! It was like I'd just passed my driving test or something - a little weird!

But others, while they were kind, said they'd pray for me, as though I had a problem. They lovingly said they'd walk through this journey with me and help me to become normal. OK, they didn't quite use those words but that is what they meant. Following my "coming out" my mental health did a downward dive. My faith wavered, my confidence plummeted and my beliefs became conflicted. I reached an all-time low, even contemplating suicide, when something inside me snapped. I knew I had to pull myself up out of this and suddenly, using all the years' experience of supporting and counselling others, I saw I had a whole toolkit at my fingers. I stepped down from my work and I surrounded myself with the people who truly loved me. I took my own advice, and sought the support of a therapist I trusted and respected. I cancelled all commitments that created any stress or worry (including my best friend's stag-do), and used the time to heal. I knew my mental health was in danger and I needed this time.

Now, I feel that I am truly living as myself. I am no longer hiding behind a false persona, wrestling with what I should or shouldn't be. Yes, I still have little wobbles from time to time – who wouldn't? But then I remind myself, God made me the way I am and He loves me, and there is nothing anybody else can do about that!

TOXIC RELATIONSHIPS

Have you ever walked away from a conversation and thought to yourself, "Wow, that person really brings the worst out in me"? You're chatting with someone you quite like, you have things in common and you are attracted to them in many ways but suddenly you find yourself drawn into the type of conversation that makes you feel uncomfortable. They're criticising and belittling someone and you find yourself laughing and perhaps even adding in your own comment. In our desire to be accepted and liked it can be easy to become blinkered to the quality of relationships that we find ourselves in. Unfortunately, sometimes we will find ourselves in friendships that ultimately are not healthy for us and certainly not confidence boosting.

This can be subtle to start with and difficult to spot, but

little by little these 'friendships' will rob us of our authentic self and decrease rather than increase our confidence. These can sometimes be called toxic relationships. When a 'friend' makes you feel bad about yourself, puts you down, manipulates you, leaves you out or behaves in a mean way towards you (either face to face or on social media) this is known as toxic behaviour. Because these behaviours can at first be quite subtle, it may be that other people notice this toxic behaviour before you do – it can be hard to hear and easier to reject their warning. But, if you are ever in doubt, go back to what a good friend looks like and check whether this relationship fits.

BITESIZE BIBLE BITS

"Do not be misled. Bad company corrupts good character."

- 1 Corinthians 15:33 (NIV)

FRIENDSHIP CHECKUP

When we feel confident and comfortable with who we are, we are less likely to accept destructive behaviour and treatment from 'friends'. Take some time to look at the people you have around you. Whether you have a large group of friends or a close few, explore what they bring to your life and what you bring to theirs. Take a moment to be grateful for your good friends - you could even tell them what they mean to you!

On the other hand, it may be that in reading this you become aware that perhaps some of those relationships are not the best for you. There may need to be a conversation, for you to distance yourself, or an assertive action to make it clear that you are not prepared to be treated in that way. This is not easy and there will be fallout. Stay strong and surround yourself with people that build you up, affirm and support you.

NIKKI'S STORY - PART TWO

If you read my earlier story, you will know that I was bullied during primary school and was so afraid of the bullies that I sided with the bully that attacked my friend. That episode haunted me so much that something in me clicked and I made the decision that no one would ever bully me or my friends again. It was scary and I had to stand up to the bully, but I discovered a little known truth. Bullies are the world's biggest cowards, and that goes for adult bullies too.

It was my first week in a new secondary school and this gang of mean looking girls began looking over at me in that conspiratorial way until one broke away with a message. Apparently, Tracy, the gang leader, wanted to have a fight with me after school. Now, I've never been a violent person, in fact quite the opposite, and things like this scare me. But, though my stomach was churning and my heart hammering, I looked the messenger in the eye and said, "Fine. Where?" The messenger trotted off and I was left alone with my friends until she returned with another message.

"Outside Woolies. Oh, and she says no kicking." I looked at the messenger a little confused, but agreed.

"Fine, I'll be there and I won't kick." The girl walked off but before the bell rang to end lunch-time she returned with another message.

"She says no pulling hair, neither."

I looked over at Tracy, surrounded by her mean gang, and she glowered at me, narrowing her eyes.

"All right, no pulling hair." I frowned at Tracy's minion. "But what sort of fight is this?"

Her friend shrugged and said, "I know, it's a bit weird but that's what she said." She swung round on her heels and returned to the gang. The bell sounded and we all piled back to class, but on the way, the messenger collared me again. "Tracy said she doesn't want to fight anymore."

I was so relieved but my face revealed nothing. "Really?" I said. "Well, that's a shame."

That story sounds really funny and entertaining now but at the time, I was really scared. However, it also gave me the confidence to stand up to more bullies, and even more so when I grew up. When I landed a job for a large corporation, (not the one when I lost a seventy-six page document!) I worked for a boss who was known as 'the bulldog'. A week into the job, he was so nasty to one of my colleagues that he reduced her to tears. After making sure she was okay, I returned to my desk and could see him tapping away on his computer, his face like thunder. I remember thinking to myself, "This man is a bully, and though working at this company looks fabulous on my CV, I can't not say anything". I distinctly remember thinking, "This is it, I'm going to say something and I might lose my job." I took a deep breath.

"Excuse me," I said. "But that was out of order. She's really upset." He glared at me, didn't say anything for ages and then spoke: "Thank you for telling me. I appreciate your honesty!" He then got up and went to apologise to the girl. I was amazed! Bullies - we must stand up to them!

FIVE GREAT CONFIDENCE BUILDING FRIENDSHIP REMINDERS

1. ENLARGE YOUR WORLD:

Expand the places you find friends. We often think that our friendships need to be formed in our place of education. This may be the case for some, but if you are struggling to find 'your people' in that setting, there are other options. Think about your interests, your skills, your abilities and find a group or a club with people of similar interests. This can be a real benefit, not only to find those people who have similar interests to you, but also to help you develop your confidence in mixing with people in different settings. There is more to life than school, and if school is a difficult place it can feel overwhelming. Enlarge your world and see that there is more.

2. FIND YOUR PEOPLE:

Choose friends based on common interests, not on popularity or social standing. Being part of the most popular group is not always what it's cracked up to be. The pressure to keep up in these groups can be overwhelming, while the rewards can be few. In real friendships, one of the most important factors is respect. Lasting friendships involve people who understand and respect each other. Friends take responsibility for one another, solve problems together and respect one another, even if they have differences.

3. PUT AWAY YOUR PHONE!

It is common for us in today's society to feel isolated and more alone than ever. Even in the age of social media, with constant digital connection, lack of deep friendships is creating a gap. Even in the age of constant virtual connectedness, we experience personal disconnectedness. We can have 'friends' on Snapchat or Instagram, we can have hundreds or even thousands of followers on TikTok, but we can still feel left out when others are having fun on Saturday night, and we weren't invited, or when someone hasn't commented on a post. It can feel overwhelming. Try to make time to see, speak and spend physical time with your friends – you could even try putting away your phones during this time too! WHAT?! I know, radical right?

4. FOCUS ON FEELINGS:

Focus on the way a friendship feels, not what it looks like. The most important quality in a friendship is the way the relationship makes you feel—not how it looks to others.

Ask Yourself:

Do I feel better after spending time with this person?

Am I myself around this person?

Do I feel secure, or do I feel like I have to watch what I say and do?

Is the person supportive and am I treated with respect?

Is this a person I can trust?

The bottom line: if the friendship feels good, it is good. But if a person tries to control you, criticises you, abuses your generosity, or brings unwanted drama or negative influences into your life, it's time to re-evaluate the friendship.

5. FRIENDS IN SEASON:

It is okay for friends to outgrow each other. People change as they find new interests, and friendship groups change as people mature. One of the most powerful friendships in the

New Testament in the Bible is between Paul and Barnabas. Together they launched the first missionary journey and they were a great church-planting team. For just over two years, they planted over a dozen congregations. On their second missionary journey, Paul suggested they take John Mark with them, and the two men had a 'disagreement' (Acts 15:36) and ended up going on separate journeys. However, despite their disagreement these two friends continued to have respect for each other. It is okay to say goodbye to friendships and develop different ones. All the friendships we had will always have played an important role in our growing up. They were great for that season, but it may be that the season has changed, and that is okay.

———

Dear Lord,

Help me to choose my friends carefully so that I can build healthy, long lasting friendships. Give me the discernment to recognise the people who are not good for me, and the wisdom to know who I can trust. Help me to be a good friend; to be kind, thoughtful, forgiving and genuine. Show me how I can be more like you.

Amen.

CHAPTER 9

My Intimate Relationships

AN INTIMATE RELATIONSHIP is when you share not only your hopes, dreams and your soul like you would with a close friend, brother or sister (philia love) but when you also share your body . You are effectively sharing all of you. Well, that's what God intends anyway. A casual sexual relationship is not His plan, because whether you like it or not, when you enter into that 'binding two people as one' (that's how it's described in the Bible), you are offering your whole self, inside and out, to that other person. Paul, one of the first Christians, warns that everyone is likely to be tempted by strong sexual desires but rather than have sex with lots of different people, it is better to choose one person and give and receive love with them. (1 Corinthians 7)

However, Paul does go on to say not everyone wants an intimate relationship, and that's ok too. (1 Corinthians 7: 32-35) Some people make the decision to dedicate their lives to the work that God has given them, allowing them to share much more of themselves with others without having a partner or family. That's a great choice for those who feel called to it. But the truth is, many of us long for that intimate connection with one other special person.

THE EARLY YEARS

When we first enter puberty, we notice body changes as we morph into adults (scary but again, perfectly normal); hair where we don't really want it; bits that grow and poke out; and other bits that seem to have a life of their own. At the time, it feels painfully embarrassing, and you wouldn't be the first to say "For goodness' sake, Lord, couldn't you have organised this in a less obvious, humiliating way?" But take comfort in the thought that we all go through it; we all have the same thoughts and fears.

Then, the hormones rush through our bodies and some of us can feel like we need to have sex RIGHT NOW. Slow down, take a cold shower, don't rush into anything. These feelings are perfectly normal too as your body is changing and stabilising itself. OK, now it sounds as though we've switched subjects and we're talking about 'My Body" again but rest assured, this is going somewhere.

These hormones are important to our intimate relationships. They will stabilise and act a bit like an antenna, seeking out our perfect partner. Sometimes the antenna might get it a bit wrong, especially in the early days, which is why we shouldn't rush into anything. But then, one day, our antenna starts buzzing, our hearts are beating and without any explanation we have fallen for a particular person and we can't think of anything else, let alone anyone else. We think of them when we're brushing our teeth, our appetites disappear, we're mooning about so much that we nearly get knocked down by a car. Slowly, as our relationship develops, we learn more about each other, trust one another, and only want to be with each other and no one else. (Yes, friends of said love-struck person, that's hard but it won't be forever, just give your lovestruck friend a bit of space and she/he will come back to you.) Before long, we make a commitment to each other.

When we were young, our churches were very strict about not having sex before marriage. Though this does seem archaic, we think they were trying to tell us: if you can wait, then wait because sex with your chosen partner can be the most wonderful feeling in the world and will cement your relationship in a special way. However there are plenty of people who have had sex with someone else before they meet "the one" and they still go on to have a strong, love-filled relationship. Remember, Jesus does not condemn us and neither should we condemn each other.

––––––

SARAH'S STORY – PART ONE

When I was a teen, my church taught heavily about no sex before marriage. I remember many youth group meetings where we would have cringe-worthy talks from well-meaning married couples telling us, 'not to touch on someone else what we haven't got.' We used to giggle and think about all the places that didn't eliminate (I've got you thinking now!) They encouraged us to read this particular book about boundaries and the dos and don'ts of relationships. What struck me was that, without exception, all the people who were feeding me this information had framed the session with 'we learnt the hard way' or 'we made the mistakes, and we don't want you to' or 'don't do what we did.' I was baffled – why should I listen to people who had not followed the rules themselves?

Now don't get me wrong, hindsight is a wonderful thing and I know without a shadow of a doubt that as a parent of a 17 year old and 14 year old, I have poured out 'well-meaning' advice that hasn't hit the spot or has sounded patronising; but my hope is that I listen and really hear what my teens are telling me.

I think there was wisdom in what those well-meaning married couples were saying. There is wisdom in waiting and not rushing into a sexual relationship. There is wisdom in honouring your body and being careful of who has access to it and when. When I look back at my youth group days, I must admit there were not many who actually managed to follow the strict advice. Some went on to have sexual partners before they were married – a few of them regretted it, others went on to be life partners, several fell pregnant and struggled through the perceived shame of the church's disapproval, but others waited. What I now know is the importance of having confidence to think carefully before acting, which is so incredibly difficult with the surging hormones.

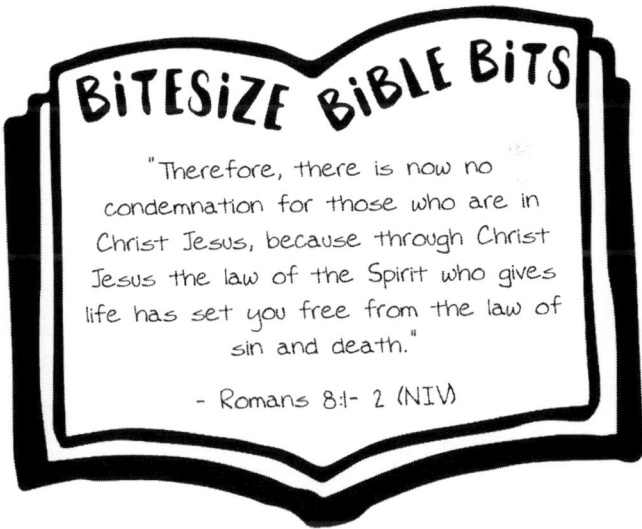

BITESIZE BIBLE BITS

"Therefore, there is now no condemnation for those who are in Christ Jesus, because through Christ Jesus the law of the Spirit who gives life has set you free from the law of sin and death."

- Romans 8:1-2 (NIV)

NIKKI'S STORY – PART ONE

I had my first proper crush when I was fourteen. I was completely head-over-heels-besotted with a man called Ivan. During a week-long, outdoor pursuits school trip (they call it PGL now) I still remember the feelings well. Hardly able to eat, I just wanted to be with him all the time, and I'm sure I was flirting very unsubtly! Honestly, thank goodness he was a good man, because he didn't encourage me (it would have been illegal if anything had happened at all). I don't even know how old he was, probably late twenties, but I didn't care. I really thought he was the one for me. He was tall, dark, had the sexiest welsh accent ever and he made me laugh. He was the funny one (in my mind anyway, I can't remember what anyone else thought). The whole year group knew, even the teachers (who thinking back probably thought this crush was quite sweet) but I didn't care. I didn't mind if anyone poked fun at me, I wanted them to know how I felt. I wanted the whole world to know how I felt. One of the tasks we had to complete was to keep a diary, and I believe Ivan was mentioned at least a dozen times on each page.

When we left Wales, I was devastated and I couldn't stop crying. I knew that nothing could come of it: after all, he was a grown man and I was only fourteen. I remember pouring my heart out to my mum and sobbing that I didn't think I'd ever meet such a perfect man again. I even taught myself the Welsh national anthem on the piano, playing it over and over again for hours. It must have been driving my family half mad, but they were surprisingly patient with me, and realised their love-struck sister/daughter would get back to her normal self eventually.

· · ·

I do believe it took me a good month to get over Ivan but even now, many years later, I remember the impact he had on me. Was I truly in love? Were those feels real? If Ivan had felt the same, could this 'love story' have had a different ending? Probably not, but at the time those feelings were real for me. I am so thankful that Ivan was a honourable man. Remember, I was fourteen! Crushes can certainly lead into dangerous territory if we take them too seriously!

CRUSHES

Well, honestly, need we say more? Most of us will have at least one crush and some of us will have many. Often, they are so unrealistic that you can recognise it as a crush but other times it might not be and – warning! – you might get hurt.

The limbic brain is the primitive part of the brain that is involved in our behaviour and emotional responses. Crushes come from this part of our brain, which is still quite dominant whilst our frontal cortex is still developing. (Our brains are not fully developed until we are 25 years old.) Our limbic brain craves dopamine (a feel-good hormone) so that's why we have crushes.

It's also very usual to have a crush on someone the same sex as you. This does not necessarily mean you are homosexual or bisexual (you might be); give it time and rather than feel you need to categorise your sexuality, trust in your antenna we spoke about earlier and let that direct you.

BiTESiZE BiBLE BiTS

"Above all else, guard your heart, for everything you do flows from it."

- Proverbs 4:23 (NIV)

SOCIAL MEDIA

Social media can be quite dangerous during a crush. Heaven knows what I might have sent to Ivan on social media! Probably many declarations of love that I would be completely embarrassed about now, or worse, pictures of myself, semi-naked. DON'T be tempted to do such things and if you have done so already, make sure you tell an adult that you trust. These things can have a nasty habit of backfiring. We all do things we regret, but it is important that we stay safe. There are many stories where girls/boys have sent pictures of themselves to someone they thought loved them back, only to find this picture is now all around school (check out some of the CEOPs e-safety stories - https://www.ceop.police.uk/Safety-Centre/How-can-CEOP-help-me-YP). Never send naked or suggestive pictures to anyone. And remember that the internet is not like Nikki's paper diary - the things you declare on there are out there forever!

————

NIKKI'S STORY - PART TWO

When I was at school, it was 'bad' to be a virgin. All the magazines told me I should be having sex, that it was the normal thing to do post 16, as long as I practised safe sex. It was all about pleasure and being 'good to myself'- Sex is great! – Have it with everyone!

But not having sex and being a virgin? Well, that meant no one fancied you, you were undesirable, you were a geek and forever destined to be alone.

Paula was in my class. She was a nice, fourteen year old girl, we weren't good friends but we were on friendly terms. She hung around with the popular girls but wasn't the most popular, if you know what I mean. She was a hanger on, quieter than the rest. I remember one morning she arrived in class surrounded by her 'friends' who were gushing in excitement. "Paula has lost her virginity!"

Pink-faced, Paula looked vaguely pleased that she was finally accepted as 'one of the gang'. Suddenly, the boys started taking an interest and for a moment I might have been jealous that she attracted all this attention. However, it was a bit short-lived. It seemed that after the boys had their 'fun' she faded from the limelight. I often wondered how she felt after that time. Did she ever regret it?

. . .

So if you're a virgin, does that mean you're undesirable and a geek, destined to be alone? I hope that by now you all know this is a load of tosh, made up by jealous, older people who had sex early on and kind of wished they hadn't, and want you to do the same so they are not alone. OK, that last bit is my own interpretation of the people who were (and probably still are) pumping that information out on social media to young, impressionable people. Sex IS great but it is greater when shared with someone you love. If you take love out of the equation you are left with nothing more than empty gratification. If you are a virgin, relax and be proud because the best is ahead of you!

NUGGET OF TRUTH

By guarding your heart, you're guarding your innermost being – your soul.

SARAH'S STORY

I had a few boyfriends and short flings before I met the 'one.' Looking back, I believe I spent a long time desperate to be in a relationship to validate my worth. If I had a boyfriend then I must be attractive and interesting enough. If someone 'snogged' me on the dance floor, then I was wanted. If I was in a relationship, I would be as good as everyone else. I guess I was scared of being left on the shelf. I was no angel and those surging hormones and poor judgement meant that I got myself into some sticky situations when it came to intimacy and physical relations (ones that I won't go into here in case my mum reads this book!). There are things I hugely regret, but I probably learnt a great deal from them too. I never want to be an adult who says "I did it, but you shouldn't"; but I do want to be an adult who can share some wisdom that comes from waiting.

My husband and I did wait until we were married for a full sexual relationship and that felt really special. We were able to really become one in all senses when we were married. This was not easy and we both pushed the boundaries that we had set for ourselves on many occasions. We certainly didn't keep to the 'sideways hugging and hand holding only in public' rule that some churches suggest! But we did decide to wait, and looking back I'm glad we did.

When Ed and I were first engaged, my university housemate said something to me that, at the time, struck me as being funny, but now is quite pertinent.

My housemate was truly a great friend. She'd been through some hard times but she always had my back and had the ability to really make me laugh. In many ways, her values and outlook on life were polar opposites to mine, but she was always there. I had led quite a sheltered life as a Christian with a metaphorical list of dos and don'ts. She, on the other hand, had a carefree attitude. She was also beautiful and got lots of attention from men. By our final year of our degree, she had a boyfriend who lived in London who travelled up regularly to visit her but there was also a stream of male visitors, night after night. Her view on intimate relationships was very different to mine and she led her life very differently.

One day, I'd returned from an afternoon with Ed and she asked me what we had been up to. As a joke I replied, "Having mad passionate sex!" To this day, her response still surprises me. She stared at me right in the eyes and said "You better not have! You have waited this long, don't go and spoil it now. You two have something special and you need to keep that."

I thought she would think our plan to "wait until we're married" laughable, prudish and antiquated but what she actually saw was something precious and to be treasured.

NUGGET OF TRUTH

Being intimate is one of the most precious connections you can have.

SAFE SEX

So, we get the message, sex is amazing when in a committed, loving relationship. However, though it would be fabulous to believe that we are all sensible, temptation-free, righteous people who never make mistakes of course that is rubbish - we are fallible. So, at least make sure you are safe. Schools offer plenty of advice about contraception. We're sure you've heard, for example, that even if the girl is on the pill, condoms also protect from disease and it's a good idea to use one.

So yes, listen to this information and learn how to be safe, even if you don't think it applies to you just yet. It's good to be prepared. But please just remember, before you jump into bed with someone, to ask yourself the question – is this God's best for me? You might find this is the safest sex of all!

———

A QUICK NOTE ABOUT ABORTION

Abortion is a terribly contentious issue with too much to say on both sides to go into it here. Whatever your beliefs about it, one thing is certain: it should not be taken lightly and it is not a casual form of contraception. We both have friends who have been through abortions and it is really tough: the process is never emotionally easy.

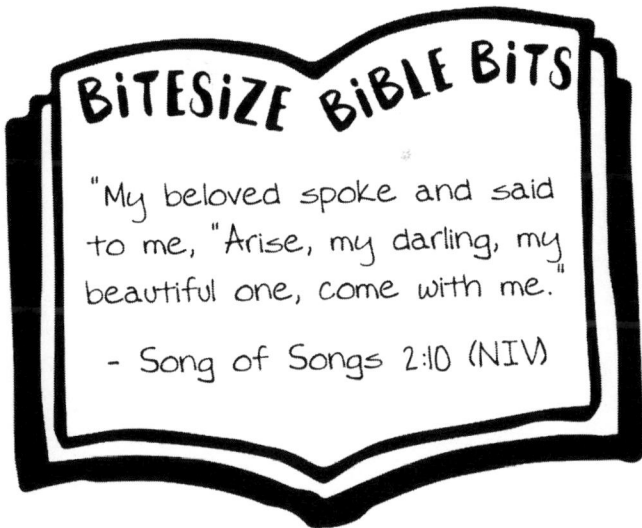

BITESIZE BIBLE BITS

"My beloved spoke and said to me, "Arise, my darling, my beautiful one, come with me."

- Song of Songs 2:10 (NIV)

ONLINE RELATIONSHIPS

The digital age means that some of us form new relationships online. Sometimes these relationships can turn into something exciting and loving, but sometimes they can turn into something dark and sinister. Somehow, it is easier to be vulnerable with someone you can't see or who is not physically in the same room as you. As parents, we are so aware of the dangers and risks young people take by 'dating' online.

Yes, it seems safer at the time, but nothing online ever goes away. Photographs, text messages, videos and audio are on the cloud forever. Even if you are communicating live through Zoom or something similar, we can never know for sure that the other person is not recording it, especially if we don't know them too well. Nor do we really know for sure that they are who they say they are. There are plenty of older men and women posing as young people to attract and elicit real young people into doing things they later come to regret.

Nikki's nephew went to school with Breck Bednar and was shocked to learn about his murder after being lured to a man's flat. Fourteen year old Breck was a normal schoolboy with lots of friends who loved playing online games. He was bright and self-aware, he had a really supportive family as well as a church family and yet he still fell prey to an online stalker who pretended to be a good friend. It could happen to anyone.

Again check out the e-safety CEOPs information, not to frighten yourself but to become armed and wise. Being informed means being prepared, and even if you believe your digital partner would never do anything to hurt you, it is wise to be aware of the potential risks you are taking.

We are on a journey of discovery, it can be exciting and wonderful but it can also end in tears. Just know that if you do make a mistake, you can come back from it, however serious. We can become stronger if we learn from our mistakes and we can help others who might be going through the same. After all, this is one of our main reasons for writing this book: to remind us that we are loved by a heavenly Father and no matter what happens, whatever bad turns we make, we can always come back to Him.

INTIMACY IS A GIFT

It is important to note that God intended us to have intimacy with each other. The Song of Songs is worth a read; you can find it in the Old Testament tucked in between Ecclesiastes and Isaiah. There are a number of different meanings that scholars have given to this mysterious book, which might not be quite what you expect to find in your Bible! But at its heart, it is a love poem between two people who are infatuated with each other. There is such beauty in giving your whole self, body and soul to the person you truly love.

Dear Lord

Thank you for the precious gift of intimacy and for showing me that I can choose who I decide to share this with. Help me to recognise the difference between real love and raw desire, and give me the wisdom to know the right time and the right person to trust with this part of me. Set your angels around me and protect me from those who will try to use me or trick me, and give me the confidence to say no when I feel pressured.

Amen

CHAPTER 10

My Family

YOU'VE PROBABLY HEARD of the old saying that goes: *You can't choose your family but you can choose your friends* – yet family is so important to our wellbeing and confidence, particularly in the early years. Family comes in all shapes and sizes, as you can imagine: we've long abandoned the idea that a family is always a mother, a father and two and a half children, like the Simpsons! There are a number of definitions online, the most common one being; 'A family is a group of two or more persons related by birth, marriage, or adoption who live together; all such related persons are considered as members of one family.' (HRSA) But we would go one step further and say, 'a family is a group of two or more people who live together as one unit.' How would you define your family?

From birth, we're entirely dependent on our care-givers and as we grow through the infant years we're like little sponges, soaking up the experiences, learned behaviours and knowledge that forms the basis of our opinions and beliefs. The carers around us really affect how we become as adults. Sometimes this is a great influence, sometimes a bad one, but most of the time it is a satisfactory influence – somewhere in the middle. Few of us come from 'perfect' families, and I would challenge anyone to define a 'perfect' family. Even our carers make mistakes – after all, they are only human!

When we get to our teenage years, the way we relate to the adults we live with alters. As we become more independent, we look for support, connection, and affirmation from other sources such as our peers, social media or other adults in our lives. However, as teens, we still need support from our own families just as much as we did when we were younger – it just might look a bit different. There are times when our families drive us completely mad: they frustrate us and certainly appear not to understand us. But don't forget, whatever age these adults may be, they have all been through the tough 'nobody understands me' years. Yes, society and culture have evolved, and developing technology has changed the way we live but that, too, has been everyone's experience: most adults have at least a twenty year age gap between their own carer and themselves, and cultural and social change has impacted every generation.

NUGGET OF TRUTH

Home is where we can take off our masks and be ourselves.

SARAH'S STORY – PART ONE

When I was much younger the dentist told me that I had too many teeth for the size of my mouth. My sister found this hilarious because I always had a lot to say. In fact, during my time at university, a lady from my church called me 'gobby.'

In many ways, my sister and I were very different. She was academically very capable and me not so much; she had a small group of close friends, and I would flit around lots of different groups. She would study conscientiously in her room, and I would be out and about generally being a bit of a show-off. But one of the main differences was the way we dealt with conflict. If an argument or disagreement happened, she would storm off, invariably slam a door, and then be silent, but I would stay to argue the point. I would go on and on and on.

My dad and I also clashed in this way. I loved a 'discussion', and my opinions and thoughts as a teenage girl were strong (that probably hasn't changed much). I always had a lot to say and was really good with my words, remembering the exact phrases people had used and catching them out on any contradictions. My dad, on the other hand, struggled to formulate what he was trying to say without becoming angry. He was really quite a fiery character and his outbursts could, from time to time, lead to plates or even chairs being thrown across the room and smashing on the kitchen floor. In general, as a teenager I wasn't much trouble,but in terms of getting my opinion heard - I did like to push it. I loved to run rings around my dad with my words and watch the result. Looking back on it I see that I probably enjoyed pushing his buttons, but at the time I thought my opinions and beliefs were ones that he needed to understand and agree with.

My mum, who hated conflict, would sit back and watch the fallout – and fallout there usually was! Reflecting back on it now, I can see that I perhaps went about it in the wrong way, but anyone who knows me knows I still love a good 'discussion'! I do, however, believe it is both important and possible to find a way of talking which allows everyone in the family to share and be open, even if it is not something they want to hear.

BITESIZE BIBLE BITS

"Children, do what your parents tell you. This is only right. 'Honour your father and mother' is the first commandment that has a promise attached to it, namely, you will live well and have a long life."

- Ephesians 6: 1-3 (MSG)

A SAFE PLACE

It seems to be a constant theme in this book - the teenage years can be a turbulent time - we are going through rapid physical, hormonal and emotional changes. We are stressed and under pressure and we need the secure and emotional base that family can provide. We need boundaries, we need to feel loved and accepted no matter what mood we are in, we need standards of behaviour, we need consistency and a place where we belong. When we make mistakes (and we will) we need a safe place to lick our wounds and be ourselves. Home.

Every good parent/carer's dream is to be told by their grown up child that they did a good job of raising them. In the middle of it all, we may not think our parents are talking any sense at all – but you never know, later in life we might actually realise they were acting in our best interest. After all, that is what good parents do; they do what they think is best for us at the time. They may not always get it right, but most of the time, they do.

Strong family relationships can go a long way to helping us grow and develop into confident adults. When life gets hard people need support from other people. Feeling accepted and understood during a crisis is a need that we all have. Families – whether traditional or chosen – can provide that. In good times and bad, our families can provide the affection and encouragement that we need and the motivation to push forward in all areas of our life.

NUGGET OF TRUTH

Whether we grow up in a 'good' or a 'bad' family, only we are responsible for our future.

NIKKI'S STORY

Like many families, my family was quite chaotic with real ups and downs. The downs were pretty terrible, on the verge of abusive, but the ups were good, sometimes even great. Now I have a family of my own, I realise how tricky raising a family is, and I appreciate that my parents did the best they could at the time.

All families struggle at one time or another, and some families struggle more than others. My birth parents divorced when I was six years old and I barely remember my father, who chose to walk away from my life and allow my stepfather to adopt us. For years, I wondered what I did so wrong that my dad chose to leave, and I was especially careful to keep my mum happy so she wouldn't do the same. However, my mum and stepdad argued terribly, and often these rows were quite violent. Believe it or not, I just took it in my stride. I remember a neighbour walking past our house just as my mum lobbed my dad's computer through a glass door.

"Is everything all right?" she asked, looking at the glass and broken computer lying on our driveway.

"Yeah, it's just mum and dad having a row," I replied and

went on playing with my younger sisters. She nodded and walked on. I was nine. Sometimes things would be a lot worse, other times better. Nowadays, I expect social services would get involved.

In my mid-teens I had everything I needed; a fabulous bedroom with my own piano, good food, siblings I got on well with, a school I loved. My parents still had extreme rows but we were used to it, and actually it often meant we had a lot of freedom. Dad didn't notice when we were out until late and mum didn't require us to do loads of jobs. We'd take the opportunity to go out for hours on our bikes, see friends and hang out with the older boys. Home wasn't always the most safe, welcoming place but my parents made sure we had a great education, they clothed and fed us well. They did the best they could and I will always be very grateful for that.

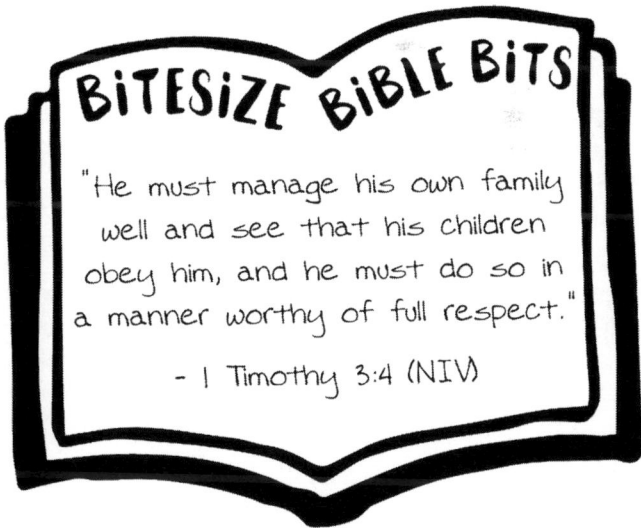

BITESIZE BIBLE BITS

"He must manage his own family well and see that his children obey him, and he must do so in a manner worthy of full respect."

- 1 Timothy 3:4 (NIV)

UNHEALTHY FAMILIES

Not all of us have had an experience of a 'healthy' relationship with our family, one where we feel safe and where we can express respect for ourselves and others. This comes from mutual trust, honesty, communication and consistency. Unhealthy relationships are ones where there is a power imbalance. Although we can all expect conflict within our families, especially through our teenage years, some people will have had experiences which have not provided those foundational things that a family should bring.

If that has been your experience of family, this is really hard but you are not alone. One in seven young people under the age of eighteen will have experienced domestic violence within the family at some point in their childhood (women-said.org.uk). 69% of the homeless LGBT young people in the UK experienced violence, abuse or rejection from their family home and 77% of those stated that their LGBT identity was the cause. (LGBT Youth Scotland 2011-21). In 2020 there were 80,000 looked after children (those in the care of the local authority and not living with their birth parents) in the UK.

Unfortunately, most adults won't change their core personality or behaviour. You may reach a point when you start to accept this and realise you may never be accepted, loved or approved of in the way you need. This can lead to extreme isolation and disappointment, and there are many adults in the world today who are still suffering from the effects of their childhood. If you have had an experience of a dysfunctional family which won't change, and is harming your life with their destructive behaviour, it is okay to cut ties. You have every right to set boundaries to protect your own wellbeing and confidence.

If any of this rings true with you, speak to an adult that you trust; and if you are so isolated you feel you don't know any trusted adults, contact Childline on 0800 1111 / childline.org.uk. They are a 24 hour helpline that will listen and give you the support you need. If you have not had the security of a supportive, loving family, you may need some external support to help you to build strong, healthy relationships in the future.

Sadly, our start in life cannot be undone and we probably will never be completely free from the pain and the trauma, though God can use our experiences to make us stronger and even help others. But, when we are older, we can heal some of the pain by the choices we make. Our carers' behaviour isn't responsible for our future decisions; we will be responsible. What happens to us in our early life is largely out of our control, but what we do in our adult lives belongs to us. We will be able to be empowered and take control.

———

SARAH'S STORY – PART TWO

In our household, we have prided ourselves in trying to have an open discussion policy, allowing all of us to question, explore and challenge, to find our voice in an ever-changing world and in our ever-changing selves. Together, we have explored belief structures and examined what we learned as children. I wanted my teenagers to know that they could voice their opinions and that I would listen; I didn't want them to have my experience with my dad, where I felt that I was fighting just to prove him wrong. I wanted my kids to know that I am unshockable, and they can come to me with anything.

How naïve of me. Of course I'm shockable!

• • •

In a conversation only this week with my daughter, who has been learning to find her voice, she asked why I would expect her to tell me everything? She explained there are some things that are incredibly hard to tell the people we love most. She asked me if I told my parents everything... of course I didn't!

My children need other people from outside of the family to share deeply personal things that they are struggling with. As a parent I am finding it hard to accept that, as my children grow into young adults, they will not only want to, but need to talk to others. I am so grateful for the people in my kids' lives who provide that listening ear: the non-judgemental sounding board, the voice of love and compassion and the non-maternal advice. My prayer is that each of us can find people who we can talk to.

NUGGET OF TRUTH

The best advice you can give a parent is to simply love. You can never love a child too much.

CASE STUDY – ETHAN'S STORY

It all started when I was around 13 years old and I was really sick with a violent vomiting bug during the night. It really frightened me and for the next few weeks I couldn't get away from the fear of being really sick. I stopped sleeping because I was so worried and my days became very difficult. I felt like I was in a dream and was too afraid to speak to anyone, especially with people my own age, although I was fine with my close friends. However, I began to have panic attacks; the worst of them were at night but I could get them in the day too.

Things got worse and I didn't want to see anyone. I even struggled with sitting on the bus and felt jealous that teens my age could speak with strangers or people they knew a little bit. I even struggled with talking to my extended family - people I thought I should be able to speak with – I found I couldn't.

My main anxiety was always related to going to bed. Around 5pm I would start to get anxious. My stomach would hurt and for years I thought I had stomach issues but no hospital could find anything. It was psychological; if I started thinking about being sick, I started to feel sick and then thought I'd really be sick. Now I know it was stress.

I never knew why this happened. It wasn't a logical thing. There was no real reason why I should feel like this; and then I worried there was something seriously mentally wrong with me. During this time, I played and wrote worship songs as an outlet.

During my second year of college, I was starting to get better. I was fed up with being the quiet one in the corner wearing dark clothes. At home, I was vibrant, lively, a completely different person but at college it was like I morphed into this anxious, scared person. However, I started to push the boat a little bit. One day, I decided not to hunch over any more. Another day, I decided to wear pink tracksuit bottoms. Slowly I became a bit more confident about who I actually am. Looking back, God was going through this with me. He was giving me the confidence to do this.

Then lockdown happened and I regressed. I was really scared of catching Covid and getting ill. Being ill is what frightened me. Also, I was really confused by all the conflicting opinions about Covid and felt very alone.

On top of this, I felt depressed because I'd finished college and I didn't know what to do with my life. I had no real direction. I was scared of wasting my life.

I started to help out with the youth pastor at my church. Then the youth pastor went on paternity leave and I was left in charge. Because I was really busy, it helped to take my mind off the worrying. The fact my days started to be a bit different also helped. But every time evening appeared, I'd feel myself getting anxious.

Leaving home and working at the church full time gave me a new confidence. Suddenly I felt I had a purpose and I was free to achieve it. I felt I could be myself and who I wanted to be.

I finally believed I'd reached a new high – the best I've ever been; confident in my work, on zoom, leading worship… I was really doing well and then I started having weird symptoms. I was so thirsty all the time. I went to the doctors who didn't seem very concerned. They took some tests and I forgot all about it. Then out of the blue, I received a phone call telling me to get to the hospital immediately. I found out I had diabetes.

I had a lot of support from my friends, family and the hospital. After the initial shock, I had a little bit of depression but soon got used to checking levels and taking insulin.

For many years I worried about getting ill. It was the worst thing that could happen to me. Now it had happened I no longer had that fear. I learned I could live with illness, it can be controlled and I realised that I can control my health and I can control my anxiety.

Every now and again, I might have a few down days but I have a relationship with God and being fully committed to Him has really helped me through. One of my favourite quotes is from film critic Mark Kermode, "It will be OK in the end. If it's not OK, it's not the end."

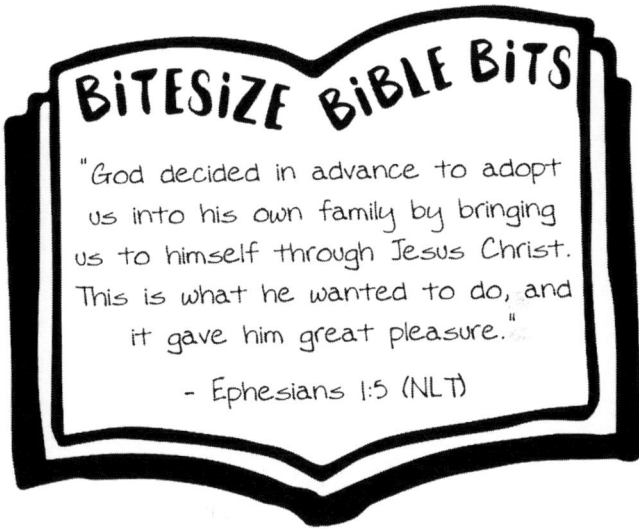

BITESIZE BIBLE BITS

"God decided in advance to adopt us into his own family by bringing us to himself through Jesus Christ. This is what he wanted to do, and it gave him great pleasure."

- Ephesians 1:5 (NLT)

GOD'S FAMILY/CHURCH FAMILY

Whether our experience of family has been positive or not, belonging to a church family as a young person can definitely add another dimension for us, especially in our teenage years. It can be wonderful to have people, other than our carers, who love us. Their guidance, encouragement and words of wisdom can benefit us hugely as it builds our confidence. I certainly know for me there were times when I listened to my church family more readily than my own family when things were particularly rough.

•   •   •

There are times when, as teens, we feel that our parents don't really understand us and our needs. Being part of a community, which hopefully creates an atmosphere where young people feel like they can be themselves is a wonderful thing. We might find that community in a club or hobby, we might be part of a sports team, but a church community is another fantastic place for us to feel accepted, supported and helped to grow in confidence of who we are and who we were made to be.

NUGGET OF TRUTH

"It takes a village to raise a child." - Old African Proverb

One of the unique things about a church is that it brings together people of all ages and backgrounds. I always imagine church like a traditional extended family: people of every generation sharing wisdom, support and inspiration with each other. The healthiest churches are the ones who have people of all ages, of all walks of life, of all cultures and social backgrounds. However, just like immediate families, churches come in all shapes and sizes and there is no such thing as a perfect church. If you choose to go to a church and become part of a church family, it should be a place that you feel loved, included and safe.

. . .

Becoming a Christian means that we are adopted into God's family as a child of God and a brother or sister to other believers. This is brilliant for us all, but especially wonderful for those who may not have had a good experience with their own birth family. Jesus calls His family to love one another.

———

NIKKI'S STORY - PART TWO

From about the age of eight, I went along to church with my sisters thanks to Mr and Mrs Man, a lovely elderly couple who collected us at 10am every Sunday morning. We piled into their tiny Vauxhall and chugged down to the church clutching our 10 pence pieces for the collection (or to spend on sweets after the service - but that's another story!) If it wasn't for them, I'm not sure we would have made it most weeks. At the time, I took Mr and Mrs Man for granted and when we moved away, I don't think we even told them! Mrs Randall ran the kids' church and I have faint memories of her giving me singing lessons once per week, free of charge. When I was a teen, Rev John Clarke and his wife Jess had an enormous influence on me. They welcomed me with open arms, were patient with me, listened to me and encouraged me. It's only many years later that I realise how much of an impact all of these people had on my faith journey, and they probably don't even realise it! God put many good people in my life to help me on my way, and even though I no longer see them they are indeed part of my own church family.

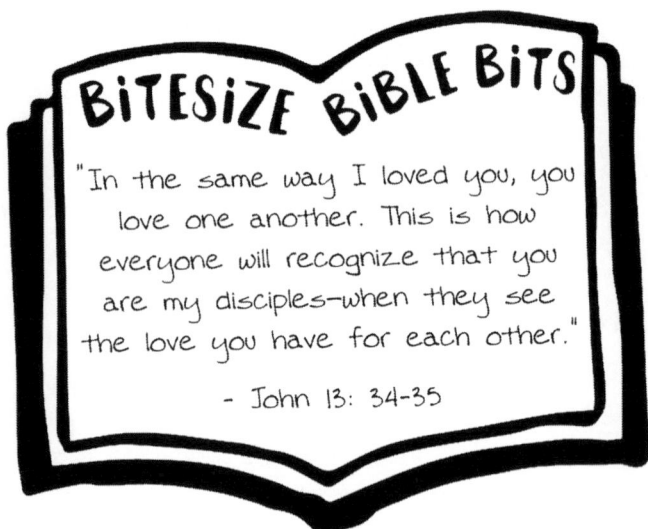

BiTESiZE BiBLE BiTS

"In the same way I loved you, you love one another. This is how everyone will recognize that you are my disciples—when they see the love you have for each other."

- John 13: 34-35

PHILIA LOVE

In the Greek language there are four words that mean 'love': philia (love between equal companions), eros (romantic love), storge (family love which includes empathy, affection and compassion) and agape (selfless, unconditional love). A church family should be one where philia love is shared. In this type of church we can share our struggles and others will help us; we can feel safe and accepted. You could join a youth or student group and enjoy journeying this tricky time of life with others who want to see you grow in confidence and faith.

FINALLY – A TOP TIP FOR FAMILY

Think about spending some regular one-on-one time with your parents/carers/family, doing something you both/all like to do. It might be watching a film, going shopping, playing a sport, walking, eating cake – whatever. Just find something you have in common, however small, and intentionally spend time together. Leave the rows and frustrations at the door. It doesn't have to be for long, but it does provide a chance to stay connected. There will be a lot that you won't agree on in life particularly during your teenage years, but finding some moments of togetherness will help maintain your relationship for your future.

———

Dear Lord

I thank you for my family and for all they do. I thank you for my church where I can connect with others and develop close relationships with people who are not in my immediate family; but I thank you mostly for you, my father in heaven, who loves me unconditionally without condemnation. Please surround me with Your people who will also love me, encourage me and listen to me. Give me wisdom to identify the people who I can trust and with whom I can be myself without worrying what they think so that I can grow in confidence and become the person you created me to be.

Amen

CHAPTER 11

Summing Up And A Last Few Thoughts

CONFIDENCE IS about believing in yourself, in your abilities and in your ideas. It lets you accept yourself for who you are, feel okay with your strengths and your weaknesses, and not want to change yourself to fit in with others. Confidence is not about being the biggest character or the most outgoing. You can be quiet or shy and still be confident. The loudest person in the room is not necessarily the most confident!

It may feel like everyone else is sure of themselves and oozing confidence, but the chances are they will have doubts just like the rest of us. The secret is understanding something fundamental – confidence is not something you have; it is something you create. Being confident is nothing more than believing in yourself. It is a sense of certainty that you can accomplish whatever you set your mind to. When you have confidence, you have the ability to take risks, think outside the box and go for the things you want in life. This is not easy, and people are lying to you if they say it is. We will all have good days and bad days. But with support and understanding we can all get there – little by little. Here are a few final pointers to help you on your way.

————

ACCEPTANCE IS KEY

According to Dr Allison Papadakis, clinical psychologist*, 'recognising that you are where you are, and you have an intrinsic worth where you are, is a really important concept.'

There may always be areas in our lives that we want to improve and change, but it is important to acknowledge that we are already awesome and as we improve, we only become more awesome. We must remember to be kind to ourselves, we need to learn to recognise and challenge our unkind thoughts. It's okay to make mistakes, it is important to forgive ourselves and ask God to forgive you too.

www.teenvogue.com/story/self-confidence-tips-for-teens

————

LET'S STOP COMPARING

It is completely natural to compare ourselves with others. It is a way that we can learn to understand ourselves and develop more of the qualities we admire, but if comparisons often leave you feeling bad about yourself, it is a sign that you may need to work a bit on your confidence. Comparing yourself to others will often take the form of negative self-talk and this will weaken and break down your confidence. Notice when your self-talk becomes negative. The only person you need to compare yourself with is the version of YOU that you want to become.

DARE TO BE THE REAL YOU

Let others see you for who you are – mistakes, insecurities, and all. Insecurities are easier to move past when we don't feel that we have to hide them. Embrace your quirks rather than trying to act like someone else, or in a way that is not true to who you are. This is why it is important to try to surround yourself with people who accept you for those qualities that you show. It may mean that you have to walk away from friendships or groups who don't allow you to be you.

———

CHALLENGE YOURSELF

Have a go at taking a safe risk. This can take many forms, maybe signing up for a school club, volunteering to help with a project, trying out for a team, entering into a class discussion more often or even talking to that person you think is cute. All of these will help to push you a little out of your comfort zone. Confidence grows with every step forward.

———

SHINE!

We are often taught to work on our weaknesses and strengthen those areas that we find difficult. This can be important when it comes to improving a grade in school, but in working on our weaknesses we sometimes forget to get better at the things that we are good at. Knowing what we are good at and moving forward with that can be a huge confidence boost.

BE WHO YOU WANT TO BECOME

Sometimes we have imposter syndrome, or we listen to the untrue belief that we are not good enough – if that happens, one way to help is to pretend! That's right, pretend. The old 'fake it till you make it' concept really does work. Embrace the idea that you are already successful, that you are already doing it. You might not be convinced at first, but eventually your thoughts will follow your emotions and you'll become a more confident person.

AND FINALLY...

Confidence levels go up and down for all of us. Sometimes, things will shake your confidence, and you must be kind to yourself when things go wrong: learn from your mistakes, think about what could be done differently and remember for next time. Perhaps you need to talk to your trusted person for affirmation and reassurance, but you should also remember all the positive things you have achieved. Don't let the disappointments put you off, but dust yourself down and have another go.

There is no magic solution that will suddenly make a person confident. But when you focus on making small, consistent steps, you will see a difference. When you feel broken or as though you don't fit into this world, you can remember the fact that God actually created you on purpose. He doesn't make mistakes. So, walk with your head held high.

"For you created my inmost being; you knit me together in my mother's womb. I praise you because I am fearfully and wonderfully made; your works are wonderful; I know that full well."
- Psalm 139:13–14 (NIV)

Further Help and Support

Action for children

www.actionforchildren.org.uk

A charity supporting children, young people and their families across England.

———

Childline

www.childline.org.uk

Helpline: 0800 1111

A free 24-hour counselling service from children and young people in the UK up to the age of 19.

Children's Society

www.childrenssociety.org.uk/what-we-do/our-work/well-being

Specific support for young people who are anxious, stressed or depressed, and for those who can't access mental health services.

———

Dove Self-Esteem Project

www.dove.com/uk/dove-self-esteem-project

Resources designed to encourage young people to develop and maintain a healthy body image during the transition to adulthood.

———

Headstrong

www.beheadstrong.org.uk

An online space for young people looking at how to get the best out of your mind from a Christian faith perspective.

———

Mind and Soul Foundation

www.mindandsoulfoundation.org

Resources, articles and teaching to encourage the church to engage with all issues around mental and emotional wellbeing.

Respect ME

www.respectme.co.uk

Respect ME has Christian values at its heart and seeks to equip, empower and build up young people to be the best they can be, breaking down the lies of the media to help them understand their value, giving them a hope and a future.

———

Headstrong – Youthscape

www.youthscape.co.uk/services/headstrong

———

Young Minds

www.youngminds.org.uk

YoungMinds Crisis Messenger – Text YM 85258

Free 24/7 support for young people across the UK who are experiencing a mental health crisis.

———

NSPCC

www.nspcc.org.uk

Helpline: 0800 800 5000

A national charity to prevent abuse, help rebuild children's lives, protect those at risk and support families.

Ollee

www.app.ollee.org.uk

A web app created by Parent Zone designed to be a digital friend for children aged 8-11 and to make a difference to their emotional wellbeing.

———

Place2Be

www.place2be.org.uk

General enquiries: 020 7923 5500

———

Anxiety UK

www.anxiety.uk.org.uk/

Helpline: 03444 775 774

———

Beat

www.beateatingdisorders.org.uk

Youthline: 0808 801 0711

Studentline: 0808 801 0811

Under 18's helpline, webchat and online support groups for people with eating disorders

———

Campaign Against Living Miserably (CALM)

www.thecalmzone.net

0800 58 58 58

Provides listening services, information and support for anyone who needs to talk, including a web chat.

Centrepoint

www.centrepoint.org.uk

0808 800 0661

Provides advice, housing and support for young people aged 16–25 who are homeless or at risk of homelessness in England.

———

FRANK

www.talktofrank.com

0300 123 6600

Confidential advice and information about drugs, their effects and the law.

———

Hope Again

www.hopeagain.org.uk

0808 808 1677

Support for young people when someone dies.

———

Hub of Hope

www.hubofhope.co.uk

A national database of mental health charities and organisations from across Britain who offer mental health advice and support.

Kooth

www.kooth.com

Counsellors available until 10pm every day. Free, safe and anonymous online counselling for young people. Check whether this is offered in your area.

———

Me and My Mind

www.meandmymind.nhs.uk

Advice and support for young people struggling with unusual experiences, such as hearing voices.

———

Mencap

www.mencap.org.uk

0808 808 1111 (Learning Disability Helpline)

Information and advice for people with a learning disability, their families and carers. Services include an online community.

———

NHS Go

www.nhsgo.uk

NHS app with confidential health advice and support for 16–25 year olds.

No Panic

www.nopanic.org.uk/no-panic-youth-hub

0330 606 1174

Charity offering support for sufferers of panic attacks and obsessive compulsive disorder (OCD).

———

OCD Youth

www.ocdyouth.org

Youth Support for young people with obsessive-compulsive disorder (OCD).

———

On My Mind

www.annafreud.org/on-my-mind

Information for young people to make informed choices about their mental health and wellbeing.

———

Papyrus HOPELINEUK

0800 068 41 41

07860 039967 (text)

pat@papyrus-uk.org

www.papyrus-uk.org

Confidential support for under-35s at risk of suicide and others who are concerned about them. Open daily from 9am–midnight.

Refuge

0808 200 0247

www.refuge.org.uk

Help and support for young people affected by domestic violence.

———

Relate

0300 003 0396

www.relate.org.uk

Provides help and support with relationships, including counselling and telephone support.

———

Rethink Mental Illness

0808 801 0525

www.rethink.org

Provides support and information for anyone affected by mental health problems, including local support groups.

———

Safeline

0808 800 5007 (Young people's helpline)

0808 800 5005 (National Male Survivor helpline)

www.safeline.org.uk

Helplines for adults and young people who have experienced sexual abuse and rape. Offers face-to-face services in Coventry and Warwickshire and another helpline specifically for male survivors.

Samaritans

116 123 (freephone)

jo@samaritans.org

Freepost SAMARITANS LETTERS

www.samaritans.org

Samaritans are open 24/7 for anyone who needs to talk. You can visit some Samaritans branches in person.

———

Shelter

www.shelter.org.uk/youngpeople

Charity working for people in housing need by providing free, independent, expert housing advice.

———

The Mix

0808 808 4994

85258 (crisis messenger service, text THEMIX)

www.themix.org.uk

Support and advice for under 25s, including a helpline, crisis messenger service and webchat.

———

Women's Aid (England)
Women's Aid Live Chat support

www.womensaid.org.uk

Information and support for women and children who have experienced domestic abuse, including support by live chat, a directory of local services and a forum.

Young Stonewall

0800 050 2020

www.youngstonewall.org.uk

Information and support for all young lesbian, gay, bi and trans people.